# Heal
# Yourself

# ANNE JONES
# Heal Yourself

## SIMPLE STEPS TO HEAL YOUR
## EMOTIONS, MIND & SOUL

piatkus

PIATKUS

First published in Great Britain in 2002 by Piatkus
Reprinted 2002, 2005, 2006 (three times), 2007 (three times), 2008,
2009 (three times), 2010

This edition published in 2012

A CIP catalogue record for this book
is available from the British Library.

ISBN 978-0-7499-4110-9

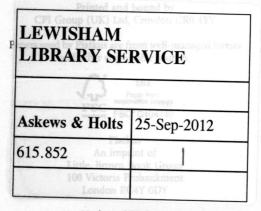

An Hachette UK Company
www.hachette.co.uk

www.piatkus.co.uk

# Contents

# Acknowledgements

To all those brave people who have been to me for healing and all those who have attended my workshops – you have all been my teachers – thank you!

To my angels in the home, Saro and Tessie, who have freed up my time in the last ten years and filled me with delicious and wholesome food.

To Apuu for showing me what determination and courage can do.

To all the Hearts and Hands teachers and supporters everywhere, including Sandra, Jen, Paru, Renee, Morna, Mincky, Pam, Suseela, Harjeet, Pete, Jeanette, Alyce, Amina, Peggy, Jackie, Annette, Marcos, Lyn, Caroline, Jasmine, Gigi, Elaine and Kirsten and all the others who have given their time, their homes and their love to make my journey an amazing and enjoyable ride.

To all my friends and family, who have accepted and supported my new beliefs.

I shall stop now before I sound like an Oscar winner!

The quotations from the Buddha which feature on the cover and at the beginning of this book are taken from *Awakening the Buddha Within* by Lama Surya Das, and are reproduced by kind permission of Transworld Publishers.

**Please take from this book that which feels good for you and leave the rest on the shelf for another time.**
**Anne Jones**


*Do not believe in anything simply because you have heard it.*

*Do not believe in traditions because they have been handed down for many generations.*

*Do not believe in anything because it is spoken and rumoured by many.*

*Do not believe in anything simply because it is found written in our religious books.*

*Do not believe in anything merely on the authority of your teachers and elders.*

*But after observation and analysis, when you find that anything agrees with reason, and is conducive to the good and benefit of one and all, then accept it and live up to it.*

The Buddha

# Letter to Readers

*Dear Readers,*

This book is a guide for your journey to inner happiness and peace. Using my own personal experiences and insights, I aim to take you to the highest point – full connection to your soul. Your soul is the fullest manifestation of your being, your highest realisation of self, so once you are fully aligned to this point your daily life and existence will take on a greater meaning. You will enjoy peace of mind and peace of heart. You will be in touch with your intuition and therefore be able to make decisions and choices that are for your highest good and greatest benefit. You will have clarity and a greater understanding of your experiences and the challenges in your life.

The journey to full soul connection is one of healing – healing the damage inflicted through this and many previous lifetimes by ourselves and others. We need to clear away the misconceptions and the emotional hurt that we have suffered. The only requirements for this journey are an intention to succeed and the patience to persevere. Like all travellers, you will suffer setbacks. You will go down paths that take you off the direct route and you will often have to travel over the same ground. The engine that will take us forward is your intention. The fuel is your attitude – positive thinking will take us a long way. Your emotional baggage will slow you down so the quicker you let this go the faster we will travel. The obstacles on your path are your fears, which we need to overcome in order to move forward.

I will lead you step by step. However, the processes I will teach you might not – and most likely will not – come naturally to you. You will find some parts easy and others will take you longer to manage. Every day you will be given opportunities to put what you learn into practice. This is the great joy of life on earth: we have an incredible opportunity here to grow and learn by overcoming the challenges and tests of our everyday lives. I won't deny that at times the process is hard. We are like onions – as we peel away the top layer of our problems, so we reveal another layer underneath. However, the rewards are high. I live in a constant state of happiness (I either feel good or ecstatic!), and I wish to share this with you. I didn't always feel this way, and it is only through constantly working on myself and my attitudes that I have reached this state, so don't give up on yourself.

It doesn't matter when you start – you can be ten or eighty years old. It doesn't matter what state of mind you are in – you can be in the depth of depression, in the deepest pit. Use this book as a helping hand to pull yourself up. The process of healing will not only help you mentally and emotionally, but will help you let go your physical problems as well.

*Best wishes and blessings for a successful journey,*
*Anne*

# Introduction

It was 1992, and a typical Malaysian afternoon. It was very, very hot and the humidity made every movement an effort. Even the geckos, the tiny but vocal house lizards that clung to my bedroom walls, could hardly raise a croak. I lay on my bed and clicked on the air conditioning with the remote control – blessed relief as the motor started to hum and cool air began to circulate the room.

I had spent my morning convincing some of the other expatriate wives of Kuala Lumpur that it was possible to type a letter on a computer and get a passable copy to paper without having a panic attack. I held these word-processing workshops most mornings in response to huge demand. Malaysian government regulations meant that we couldn't work so we all had plenty of time on our hands. Many of my students were trying to catch up with their children who, cruising in technology's fast lane, were making mum feel like a dodo.

It was tiring work and I was taking a well-earned rest

after lunch before intending to return to my PC to continue with the preparation of the next *Expatriate* newsletter. My life was full, interesting and stimulating and I was as happy as I had ever been. Little did I know that my whole existence was to change dramatically and mystically that day – in fact, that life would never be the same again!

As I closed my eyes, I could hear the faint sounds of the kitchen staff clearing away lunch and the muted call of a bird in the lush tropical vegetation outside my bedroom window. I was relaxed and soothed by the hum of the AC. Then came the voice. It penetrated all the vague thoughts and half ideas moving through my head. It was persistent and strong. It certainly couldn't be ignored! 'Isn't it time you started healing?' the voice asked me. 'What do you mean?' The tone became more determined: 'Start healing.' 'How?' Now I was confused. 'Speak to Sal,' came the reply. End of conversation.

I sat bolt upright. I could hardly believe what had just happened, but I felt a great well of excitement, and a tremendous buzz started to rush through my body. Yes, yes, yes! Although healing was the very last thing on my mind – and I had minimal experience of the world of psychic phenomena – I knew that this was something I had to do. Wow! I thought about Sal, the lovely English lady who wrote the restaurant reviews for the newsletter. Someone had once told me that she was a powerful spiritual healer.

As I sat there thinking about the possibility of my being able to heal, I felt happier and happier – what a wonderful prospect. I remembered how, many years before, my mother had broken her ankle and had been laid up for some time with a complex fracture. One day I had put my hands on her leg and she had told me that they were hot – she said she could feel the heat even through the plaster. I continued to sit with my hands on her ankle for some time.

When she went for her next check-up and the doctor pronounced an unexpectedly fast recovery, we had remembered my 'hands-on' experiment and wondered if this had had anything to do with it. But it was a one-off experience; I soon put all notions of healing to the back of my mind as I rushed on with my life as a computer sales and marketing executive.

Although not particularly religious, I had always believed in the force of GOOD and that there is a reason for everything – 'fate', I used to call it. I also knew that my mother's mother, who had died before I was born, was in some way in contact with me. She had intervened to help me in the past when I had been in danger, and she seemed to have a significant knowledge of me and my life. One particular event I recall occurred when I was speeding along in the fast lane of a motorway. Suddenly I heard my grandmother's voice telling me to pull in. I did as I was told – and was saved from certain collision with a large lorry that, just moments afterwards, spun out of control from the middle to the outside lane. Thank you, Grandmother!

So when the voice spoke to me that afternoon in Kuala Lumpur, I recognised my grandmother, telling me something important once again. This strong and forceful lady was not to be ignored. The next day I saw Sal at a social gathering. I walked up to her and said, 'Sal, I have to talk to you about healing.' Her face was all smiles and she gave me a knowing look. 'I'll send a book around to your house later today,' she told me. 'Read it. As you read it you will feel that you already know the contents. Then start healing!' She made it all sound so simple.

That afternoon I received a copy of *Mind Magic* by Betty Shine, and the following day I left for a four-week holiday in England and France. I read the book on the plane. Just as Sal had told me, the words were completely familiar. (I have bought many copies of this wonderful book since and passed them on to budding healers.) Once on holiday, I started practising the simple process that Betty teaches on my family and friends. I had enough 'ooh, that's good', 'your hands are so hot', 'my neck feels better', and so on to make me confident that I was having some effect.

On my return to Kuala Lumpur, I arranged a lunch date with Sal. I drove over to her house full of antici-pation and excitement. As I walked through her front door, her eyes crinkled and she pronounced, 'You're healing, it's in your aura.' Wonderful news – she could see the change in my energy field and it was just the proof I needed. Later, I told her more about the afternoon of my grandmother's visit and she was able to tell me that some weeks before she, too, had had a visit from my grandmother, during one of her meditations. My grand-mother had told Sal that I would be making contact, and had asked Sal to help me on my way, telling her not to phone me but to wait for me to come to her.

From that time on, I was convinced that healing was my new path and I began to get more messages from my spiritual guides. My grandmother was joined by an angel called Sharma and a Native American called Yellow Hawk. The three of them would appear in my mind's eye during my meditations and I would listen to them talking to me in my head, rather like very loud thoughts. They advised me to give up the workshops and the work on the newsletter and to concentrate on healing. I followed their advice and was amazed by the way in which people immediately came into my life to take over these tasks. It was the beginning of a trend that has continued to this day: I always meet the people I need at the time that I need them.

My new life had begun. I took over the small guest bedroom and bought a massage table to use as a healing bench. My guides showed me how to sweep through the energy around a patient – this clears away any misaligned energies that may be inhibiting the natural flow. When our energy levels are depleted we are likely to feel depressed, and our physical body is likely to become sick, so the second stage of the healing process is to energise. I was taught to tap into the unlimited source of life force energy that surrounds us, and utilise this to raise the energy levels of those who are mentally, physically or spiritually in need.

One of the most significant things I learned in those early days was that healing – the channelling of universal healing energies – varies in its effect depending on the recipient. The healer can pass on the energy but it is up to the patient to use this energy in the way they consciously or subconsciously think fit. In actual fact, each person heals him or herself. I noticed that some people would be well for a time and then come back a few months later with the same problem. After a while, I realised it was usually due to their attitude to life. The people who managed to stay well after treatment were mainly those who were determined to get well and had a positive, upbeat approach to life, free from unnecessary worry or fear. Those people who had negative emotions such as anger, hate or guilt, or who lacked self-esteem, would get sick again. To help these patients, I researched and experimented with different self-healing techniques and started to keep notes of those that worked for most people.

I very soon had another message: this time to formulate workshops to pass the healing skills I had learned on to others. I included all the exercises and self-healing methods that my patients had been using, as my ex-patients told me constantly that they had revolutionised their lives and given them incredible feelings of self-empowerment. I have been giving these workshops around the world for the past four years. More recently, my voices have been telling me to write books, in order to pass these skills on to an even wider audience.

I have discovered that there is a reason for everything in life and behind every illness there is a cause. Poor mental and physical health is the result of one's attitude, other people and the challenges that life brings. I have seen so many people weakened and debilitated by the effects of physical and emotional trauma caused by accidents and other people. Often these emotions stay bottled up inside us and, over time, this old emotional baggage can have harmful effects.

The good news is that once we acknowledge the underlying cause or the root of the problem, our healing can begin. If we change our negative attitudes and thinking patterns and release the pent-up emotions of the past, we will either start to get better by ourselves, or circumstances will draw us towards someone who can help us.

As a healer I know that for a successful transformation and healing I need to find the root cause of the illness that is troubling my patient. When I have discovered the source of the problem, I can release the energy that created the physical or mental malfunction. I believe that this is the most important aspect of the healing process. In this book I shall help you to find the cause, the root, the source of your own problems. We are beings of energy and therefore we need to heal our energy body before our physical body will respond. In ninety per cent of the cases I treat, the source of illness and unhappiness is attitudes, thought processes and emotions – our own and those of the people with whom we share our lives.

By using simple exercises we can re-energise our bodies and release the blocks that stop us getting the very best from our lives. I shall show you how to reprogram your thoughts, your attitudes and mind-set to create a more healthy and happy life. I shall also show you how you can become less affected by other people and be more at ease with your own decisions and your own needs. It will take work on your part and, in some cases, it may take some time before this new way of looking at life will kick in and affect your health. Of course, it may be that your physical body has deteriorated beyond the point of repair, or that you have an illness that is your 'exit plan' from this lifetime. In these circumstances your healing will be of the spirit. You will find peace of mind and strength to cope with your illness and the days ahead.

I also think it is important for us to realise why we are here and the purpose of life. Once I understood that there is a reason for everything, I was able to cope far more easily with my experiences and events in my life. I have therefore included my perception of the meaning of life: why we suffer, what happens when we die and the role of faith in our lives.

Over the last few years, my guides have shown me how to work with energy and pass this vital commodity on to others. As well as revealing the healing process, they have shown me the powerful ancient symbols that can invoke the energies for even the most sceptical. I explain the healing process in the book so that you, too, can tap into the vast source of life force. You will also find the healing

symbols throughout – use them on yourself to raise your
energy levels to fight illness and to lift yourself out of
despondency and depression.

I have included exercises in each chapter to help you
with your healing. Many of these are visualisations – a
form of meditation – and you may find it helpful to record
them on to a tape, or memorise them, or perhaps get a
friend to read them out for you. Alternatively, you can
purchase a CD of the meditations from the Hearts and
Hands healing organisation (for contact details, *see page
260*). Give yourself time to do these meditations and find
a quiet space for yourself, with the phone switched off
and the children safely elsewhere. When using the symbols,
trace them in the air in front of you – don't worry if they
are not exact, they don't need to be. Once you have traced
them, put your hand on yourself wherever the healing is
needed and the energies will flow automatically.

Let us begin our journey with a look at how our energy
system works.

# I

# Our Energy System

In this chapter, we explore the energy body. We access the energy flow using a healing symbol, and use meditation to balance our energy centres. We see how positive and negative thoughts can affect our energy levels and our health, and look at ways to protect ourselves from other people's bad 'vibes'.

Are you searching for happiness and contentment? Are you merely dissatisfied with your lot in life, or do you have a particular physical or mental problem that you would like to heal? If you are suffering in any way, I invite you to journey with me through the pages of this book where I shall share with you the insights and knowledge that have helped so many people to well-being. I shall show you a philosophy and way of living that will enable you to create your own happiness and health. You will become a master of life, not a victim. You will be in control, not controlled. You will be empowered, not weakened. You will gain self-respect and a love for life. Does that sound appealing? Are you up for it? Then let's go . . .

## *Meditation*

I am a great believer in meditation. Since I was 'awoken' to healing I have meditated regularly. I find it has many benefits, not the least of which is the peace and calm it brings. I am able to relax in a way that I was never able to before. I used to be a compulsive doer and achiever and relaxing was not in my vocabulary. Since I have learned the art of stillness, my health has improved dramatically. I am no longer plagued with migraines and my nervous and acidic stomach problems have almost entirely disappeared.

Like most Westerners, I found the Buddhist method of meditation – clearing the mind of everything and moving into the void – rather difficult. My mind would flutter like a butterfly from one subject to another: planning menus for the weekend, thinking of my family, generally working through projects on my to-do list. So I adopted the easier and less demanding method of guided meditation. This way someone leads you through a story line and you follow with your imagination. It gives you something to focus on, and some healing processes are usually included within the meditation.

Many of the exercises in this book are forms of guided meditation, and are available on CD from the Hearts and Hands healing organisation (for contact details, *see page 260*). You may find it beneficial to get together with a group of friends and meet regularly to do the meditations together, in which case you can also request a meditation pack for group meetings. If you don't have the

CD, you can record the meditations yourself on to a cassette and play them while you close your eyes and follow. Allow plenty of pauses to let your mind and imagination wander. These pauses can be as long as you need them to be, providing you don't find yourself losing the thread of the meditation. If you find it difficult to visualise clearly, don't worry. Just follow the words anyway, and you will still benefit simply by focusing on them.

## Preparation for meditation

- Find a quiet place in your home away from the children and pets.
- Turn off the phones.
- Make yourself comfortable: take off your shoes and make sure your back and neck are supported (if you can manage it, you can sit in the yoga lotus position, but it is not necessary for this type of meditation).
- Drop your shoulders and focus on yourself. Let go all your responsibilities and cares and allow this time to be just for you.

I would like to introduce you to a simple meditation to help you relax – follow this short breathing exercise and you will be surprised how easy it is to let go of tension.

---

EXERCISE: BASIC BREATHING TO ASSIST RELAXATION

- You can do this exercise anywhere, at any time that you need to relax (apart from while driving the car).
- Close your eyes and drop your shoulders.
- Breathe in deeply four times – breathing deeply into your stomach.
- As you breathe in, visualise a beam of white light entering the top of your head.

- As you continue to breathe, see the light moving down into your body: through your head, your neck and down through your chest, stomach, legs and feet.
- See the light travel through to the ground beneath you.
- Follow the light into the very centre of the Earth.
- Feel yourself completely relax for a few moments.
- Slowly open your eyes and rejoin your surroundings.

---

Now you are relaxed I suggest you find yourself some paper and a pen. There will be more exercises to perform as we go and you may want to take notes of certain points. You may even want to create a special healing journal. If the thought of writing seems too tiresome – or the effort of finding a pen too much! – you can always take your notes mentally. Start by 'writing down' what you would like to heal or improve in your life.

Maybe you suffer from anxiety. Do you worry a lot? Do you have migraines? Do you suffer from arthritis, kidney stones, high blood pressure, cancer, or a heart condition? Whatever it is, jot it down. Do you know why you suffer from these ills? You may feel that life has dealt you a bad hand or that your illness is genetic and inherited from your family (don't worry if you haven't a clue at this stage). Whatever you feel might be the reason or reasons, write it down. I shall ask you later to refer back to what you have written.

Your healing process started at an unconscious level as soon as you picked up this book, as this was a sign that you are prepared to become responsible for your health and well-being. To begin the process consciously, I would like you to open your mind and take an open attitude to what I am about to tell you. I shall begin by explaining how your body works on an energy level and why we get sick.

## *Our Energy Body*

Before we can consider how the healing process works we need to explore our anatomy at the energy level. We each have an energy field, or 'aura', around our physical body. Our aura is egg shaped and can extend as far as 2 metres around our body. (In fact our whole body is energy, but for the purposes of this explanation I shall differentiate between our physical body and our energy body.)

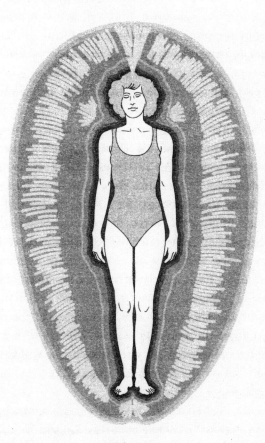

*The Aura*

Our aura is connected to our spiritual body. It joins us at birth and leaves our physical form at death. It is a continuous stream of energy that flows through and around our physical body.

Apart from reflecting your physical and mental state, your aura is also illuminated by the state of your soul – your spirit, the invisible but highest form of your being. You will have seen paintings in churches and cathedrals where Jesus and the angels have golden halos that depict their purity of spirit. In India the process of pranic (energy) healing has been followed for centuries. The philosophy behind this healing technique is based on cleansing and energising the aura to achieve perfect health.

In China, where the energy body is called 'chi', there are several methodologies and healing techniques that clear and energise the aura. The one currently gaining popularity in the West is tai chi, an ancient practice of raising and smoothing the flow of one's energy. The Native Americans shake rattles and bang sticks to break down blockages in the aura flow, then spin them clock-wise to bring in the energy. So despite the general lack of perception of it in the West, the concept of the aura has been accepted in many cultures for thousands of years.

Every living thing has an energy field: every animal, tree and plant has a clearly defined aura. When a branch of a tree is removed, its energy field will still be in place for some time afterwards, like a phantom of the original limb. At first the rest of the tree will try to repair the missing part, but eventually the tree's aura will retract to take the form of the remaining shape. The same happens with humans.

I was once called to the bedside of a man who had had a leg amputated following gangrene caused by diabetes. His relatives had asked me to visit him as he was in severe pain. The pain he felt was coming from the leg that had been amputated and was particularly severe in his missing foot! No matter how many drugs and pills he was given the pain persisted. It only took me a few moments to bring the aura of his missing leg back in line with the rest of his body, and immediately his pain disappeared. The story illustrates the strong connection between our energy body and our physical body.

Although most of us don't see auras on a day-to-day basis, they were definitely recognised by the painters of the past. When I visited the cathedrals of Moscow I was overwhelmed by the beauty of the icons and frescoes. Every single religious being, be it a saint or an angel, was shown with a bright golden halo – which is, of course, the aura that shows so strongly around the head. Purity of thought is reflected in the aura so these highly evolved beings naturally have a clearer and brighter halo than most of us earthly mortals! You might like to try this little exercise to see if you can detect a friend's halo.

---

EXERCISE: SEE THE AURA
- Get a friend to sit in front of a blank wall, preferably a cream or white one.
- Turn down the lights.
- Close your eyes.
- Open your eyes and squint a little. Do you see a bright rim around your friend's head?
- Now look beyond their head – as though you are seeing through them. If you can see colours appearing around them you are seeing their full aura – well done! If you can't, never mind, keep trying!

---

## The energy flow

So to recap, our aura is a moving flow of energy that moves constantly through and around our body. Let's now see if we can feel it for ourselves. One of the easiest places to connect with the energy flow is through the energy centres in the palms of our hands. Healers use these outflow points to pass energy to their patients. Follow this simple exercise to find out whether you, too, can feel the energy flowing.

---

EXERCISE: FEEL THE FLOW OF ENERGY THROUGH YOUR HANDS

- Rub the centre of each of your palms hard with your thumb.
- Hold your hands opposite each other.
- Feel the energy pulsing, and move your hands in and out to increase the effect. You may also feel a tingling sensation in your hands.

---

## Accessing the energy stream

Feeling the flow of energy is the beginning of a process that enables access to a great source of life force energy, which can be drawn on to replenish energy reserves when they are depleted. If you feel tired or run down, you are suffering from depleted energy. If this situation is allowed to continue, you could end up with a lowered resistance to germs and viruses and, ultimately, a depressed immune system.

The process is simple and can be practised by anyone. To help you overcome your doubts and any mistrust you have of your abilities, I have a symbol that will invoke the energy stream for you. It really is very simple – the symbol is powerful and will do the work for you!

**HEALING SYMBOL**

This is the main healing symbol and will invoke the universal energies of love and compassion, which are those of the highest vibration. The energy will replenish your life force energy reserves and help raise your immune system. It will also give you a spiritual lift.

*Trace the symbol in the air in front of you, using your hand or finger. Start on the right-hand side and finish with the dot.*

---

EXERCISE: USING THE HEALING SYMBOL

- Find a quiet space and relax.
- Close your eyes and visualise yourself surrounded by white light. If you can't see it, don't worry – the intention will be good enough.
- Trace the healing symbol in the air in front of you three times, starting from the right side and finishing on the left, making the dot last of all. You can draw with your finger or your whole hand. Use whichever hand feels most comfortable.

- Place your hand on any part of your body that feels tense or that hurts, and let the energy flow.
- If you want to simply boost your general energy reserves, place your hand on top of your head.
- If you are feeling sad, place your hand on the centre of your chest.
- If you are feeling nervous, place it on your stomach – your solar plexus.
- Breathe in deeply and hold your hand in position as long as you wish.

---

These are the sensations you may experience when using the healing symbol:

- Your arms may feel heavy as it makes you relax.
- Your tummy may gurgle as the energies activate your gastric juices.
- You may feel tingles in your arms, hands, legs, feet or anywhere in your body as the energy flows.
- You may feel a surge of happiness as this high vibration energy gives you a lift.
- You may feel peaceful and calm.
- Any pain you are suffering may be alleviated, although sometimes it gets a little stronger before it disperses.
- You may feel warmth coming from your hand – this is the energy creating heat.

This flow of energy will raise your energy levels and uplift you mentally, emotionally and physically. It will also revitalise your aura – let me tell you a little more about this energy field, which has such an impact on our health and wellbeing.

Your aura is never static. In a healthy and balanced

person it flows directly from the head all the way down, back up through the centre of our body to our head and back down and around again in a continuous stream. It supplies a constant flow of energy through our energy lines – the meridians – to all our vital organs, so keeping them healthy. These meridians work in the same way that blood vessels and arteries do to send blood to all parts of a healthy body. If an organ is depleted of energy then it will eventually become sick, as has been proved through the use of modern scientific instruments that are able to read extremely fine differences in energy.

When I was in Hong Kong in 1997 I had my energy levels read and balanced by one such machine, called a bio-resonator, and I am told that alternative medical practitioners in Germany use these quite extensively for diagnosing organs with low energy.

If your whole body is low in energy then your immune system becomes weak, and you will be liable to catch any bug around. Many diseases are directly connected to a breakdown of the immune system. Myalgic encephalomyelitis (ME) and AIDS are two that come immediately to mind. ME in particular often manifests as low energy. Although the condition is caused by a virus, it can be related to stress and overwork, both common causes of energy depletion.

Our aura is changing shape and colour all the time. I occasionally get a clear view of this when I am healing someone. The diseased part of the body will have muddy and dull tones and the rest will be moving and changing colour constantly, along with changes in the person's thoughts and emotions. In some ways I am glad that I can't see this colour change all the time, although I have often envied the abilities of my friends who can. It would be most disturbing to watch people continually changing

colour like chameleons and, of course, if anyone were
angry or upset with me, there would be no hiding the fact
as their aura would go a wonderful tomato red!

## Reading the aura with Kirlian photographs

The Russians have developed what is known as a Kirlian
camera, which can photograph auras. You will find these
cameras set up in many New Age or crystal shops in the
high street, and at body, mind and spirit fairs around the
country.

If you have your photograph taken you will usually
receive a short text describing the state of your aura and
your probable current state of mind. Remember, though,
that your energy field is constantly changing in line with
your mental and emotional state. The colours that are
picked up by the camera – or by yourself if you manage
to see them – reflect the emotions and thoughts of the
moment.

Here are some examples:

| | |
|---|---|
| **Red** | Anger, strength, power, vitality. |
| **Blue** | Intuition, communication. |
| **Purple** | Spiritual attainment, mystical under-standing, enlightenment. |
| **Green** | Mid-green: healing and calming; light green: versatility; dark green: jealousy. |
| **Indigo** | Wisdom, inspiration, creativity. |

If you look carefully at a Kirlian photograph you will see
some blobs of light running down the centre of the figure.
These blobs of light are energy centres, which we refer
to as 'chakras' (the word chakra means 'spinning wheel'

in Sanskrit). There are many chakras on our body and it is at these points that the energy flows from the energetic body to the physical body, feeding our whole being with life force.

## The Chakras

There are seven main chakras on our body. The state of our chakras determines the flow of energy to our body and it is therefore imperative – for both our health and our emotional stability – that they are kept in perfect harmony and condition. For fully effective functioning, the chakras should be open and spinning in a perfect circle, in a clockwise direction.

A chakra can be damaged by an emotional experience or trauma – we refer to ourselves as 'heartbroken' when we have lost someone we love, and this truly reflects the condition of our heart chakra, which monitors and maintains not only the physical condition of our heart but all the emotions related to love. The pain we feel from heartbreak is a true pain, caused by a tear in the chakra.

The following illustration shows you where the chakras are found and hence which physical parts and organs of the body they affect. You can also see which emotional aspect they control. Their different colours encompass the complete spectrum and each colour has its own vibration and energy pattern, which links into the emotions related to the place on the body where the chakra sits.

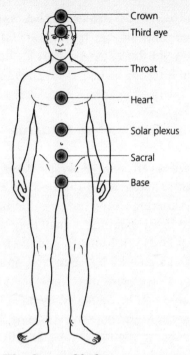

*The Seven Chakras*

As most of us cannot see our chakras and it takes time and practice to be able to sense the state of them, I have found the use of a pendulum invaluable for assessing whether they are damaged or depleted. A pendulum is any weighted object that has been attached to a piece of thread, cord or chain, and it can be used for dowsing, the ancient method of sensing energy, water, minerals and so on. You can use a crystal, metal or wooden drop or buy a pendulum from a New Age or crystal shop.

EXERCISE: CHECKING YOUR CHAKRAS
You will need someone to help you with this exercise. Use a pendulum with a thread length of about 20 cm.

- Lie down on the floor and ask your friend to hold the pendulum over each of your chakras. Watch the way the pendulum swings.
- If the chakra is balanced and healthy, the pendulum will swing in a good-sized circle (about 15 cm or more in circumference).
- If the chakra is out of balance, the pendulum will swing either in a smaller circle – showing that the chakra needs energising, or elliptically – showing that it is damaged in some way.

---

## Chakras and our emotions

Emotional experiences and thought patterns can affect the chakra system and disturb the balance and harmony of these spinning vortexes of energy and light.

### Crown

Disbelief in God, lack of faith or any spiritual under-standing will make the crown chakra small and closed down. Conversely, a great spiritual experience of joy will open this chakra up. By using the pendulum to check, the students in my healing workshops notice that they have much larger crown chakras at the end of our time together, after focusing on their spiritual aspects.

### Third eye

This chakra is the one that Indian women cover, especially when they are married, to prevent them being affected by the thoughts of others – men's carnal intentions, I suppose! If you are visualising through meditation or generally following your intuition, this chakra will be open. If you are psychic it will also be big and strong. If you have no sense of 'other worldliness' – i.e. you only believe in what you can see and touch, then your third eye chakra may be slightly smaller than your others.

### Throat

I have seen this chakra closed down in people who cannot speak their true feelings, or who have been silenced for cultural reasons. If you are in a relationship where your views are never listened to or you cannot express yourself, the health of this chakra will be threatened. However, a singer or an actor, or anyone who uses their voice actively and well in their work, will have a huge circle of blue.

### Heart

Loss or separation from a loved one will damage this chakra, hence the expressions 'heart torn', 'heartbroken', and so on, as already discussed. Newly weds or people who spend their lives loving and caring for others will have large green energy centres. Although the heart chakra is normally green, it is often seen as pink because this colour is the vibration of love and compassion, and this is the chakra that receives and gives out love.

### Solar plexus

Our solar plexus, just beneath our lungs and diaphragm, is where we store those emotions we haven't let go. If we have anger, guilt or loss that we haven't worked with and released, then this chakra will be affected. The solar plexus is where we feel the wobbles of nerves, the butter-flies that come to the surface when we are anxious – so any nerve-wracking experience will throw this chakra out of kilter. We also pick up other people's emotions here, as this chakra is extremely sensitive to the energies that are around us.

### Sacral

This chakra relates to our sexuality and if you have problems in this area of your life, the chakra will be affected, particularly in women. The sacral chakra is also the source of our creativity, so if we are painting, writing or creating in any way it is likely to be balanced. For the same reason, this is the chakra where writer's block resides. The sacral chakra is affected by our value of ourselves. If you have problems believing in your self-worth then it will be distorted. It is also affected by our attitudes and patterns of behaviour.

### Root

This one is often referred to as the 'base' chakra. In men, it reflects their sexuality (careful with the pendulum here, ladies!). It also reflects how secure you are feeling. Someone who has just lost their job will have a small base chakra. When I moved from Hong Kong to live back in the UK my base chakra was small for some time, until I settled into a new location and put down roots. Anyone who spends too much time daydreaming and is not grounded in the reality of life will have a small base chakra. Attention deficiency problems in children will also be reflected in this chakra.

I mentioned earlier that our chakras should be symmetrical and spinning in balance (a perfect circle) for our energy to be free flowing. I have found the following meditation exercise is really effective in repairing and perfecting their shape and spin.

All you need for this exercise is a quiet place, and you

can let your imagination do the rest for you. You will find it calming and relaxing, and I recommend you make it part of your morning routine – it only takes about ten minutes.

---

EXERCISE: BALANCE YOUR CHAKRAS

- Find a quiet place where you won't be disturbed. Close your eyes and breathe in deeply four times. Imagine that you are sitting in a beautiful rose garden. Feel the cool grass beneath your bare feet.

- You have in your hand a delightful rose of deep rich red. As you look at this rose, it begins to spin and create a perfect circle of red light. As you look at this strong red disc, think of the base of your spine. You feel secure and strong.

- Pause for a few moments while you visualise the red light. Let yourself be absorbed by the red light. Now change your focus to look at an orange rose. Watch the orange rose as it spins into balance and creates a brilliant orange disc.

- Your orange sacral chakra is the seat of your sexuality. Feel positive; feel your creativity flow; feel yourself enveloped in orange light.

- Pause for a few moments while you visualise the orange light and let yourself be absorbed by it. Look at a yellow rose and see it spinning brightly and perfectly into a completely balanced circle.

- Visualise your solar plexus. Let go of your anxieties and fears and see the yellow disc getting larger and clearer.

- Pause for a few moments while you visualise the yellow light and let yourself be absorbed by it.

- You are now holding a rose of purest pink, the colour

of love. See it spin and become a perfect circle of pink light.

- Feel your heart centre; see pink light pouring in and out as you open yourself to the free flow of love in your life.

- Pause for a few moments and let yourself be absorbed by the pink light. You are now looking at a blue rose. Watch the rose as it spins and turns into a perfect circle of blue light.

- As you look at this bright disc of blue, think of your throat. Know that you can speak your feelings and speak your mind as this perfect blue circle grows bigger and stronger second by second.

- Pause for a few moments and let yourself be absorbed by the blue light. You are now holding a rose of deep blue tinged with purple – indigo, the colour of the deepest ocean.

- The rose starts to spin into a perfect circle of indigo light. Connect with your third eye. Let yourself be open to all your natural gifts: your intuition, your natural healing abilities, your psychic powers.

- Pause for a few moments as you let yourself be absorbed by the indigo light. Now you are holding a rose of the very deepest purple. This is the most perfect rose of all.

- As you look at the rose, it begins to spin, and as it spins you see white light pouring out from the centre of the circle. Feel the connection to your crown and sense your closeness to the divine. Open yourself to the essence of your spirit – feel the divine within you.

- Pause while you let yourself be absorbed in the white light.

- See all the colours of your chakras blending together, then see the circles getting smaller and turning back

　　into roses. Feel total balance and harmony sweep over
　　you.
- Slowly come back into the room but continue to asso-
　　ciate with this state of balance and harmony.

---

After a while you will be able to 'manage' your chakras
and keep them clear and open – just visualise them in
your mind's eye, then see them spinning. Whatever you
are going through, you will be able to take some control
of how it affects your wellbeing.

Now I suggest you use the healing symbol on each of
your chakras to complete their healing. By healing the
chakras you affect not only the physical body around them
but also the emotions and senses attached to each particular one. Draw the symbol three times over each chakra
and then let the energy flow – raise your hand up and
down slowly about 10 cm. Afterwards you can check your
chakras again with the pendulum. See the effect of the
healing you have given them with the meditation and the
healing symbol.

We shall now look at the way other people's fears, behaviour and attitude can deplete our energy, and discover
ways that we can protect ourselves from their negative
thoughts and neediness.

## Avoiding Energy Thieves!

Have you ever spent an evening with a friend who was
going through a hard time and felt completely drained
on your arrival back home? This is because you have been
literally drained of energy. If someone is depressed, their

energy levels are depleted because they are in a negative emotional and mental state. They know subconsciously that they need to raise their energy levels, so when a friend comes through the door they immediately latch on to them and extract as much energy as they can.

Of course, we are only too delighted to help out a friend in need and, once in a while, we can afford to give up some of our life force. However, if this happens on a regular basis, you will find that your own vital energy resources become depleted and you may eventually become sick yourself. Perhaps you work with someone who is always downhearted, who is always moaning and seeing the worst in every situation. Office gossip, too, is generally a negative pastime – after all, it's much more fun to find fault in others than to talk about the good things they are doing. Whether they realise it or not, the office misery and the office gossip are stealing your energy.

## Using the egg

For your own benefit, it is best to try to avoid those people who leave you feeling drained. If this is impossible, here is a simple exercise that you can follow which will protect you against the emotions and attitudes of other people.

---

EXERCISE: PROTECT YOURSELF FROM OTHER PEOPLE'S EMOTIONS – THE EGG

- Find a quiet space and close your eyes.
- Imagine there is a large egg in front of you with a door.
- Enter the egg through the door and then shut the door behind you.
- Notice that the walls of the egg are very thick and

that nothing – but nothing – can penetrate these walls except love.

- Know that the emotions, thoughts and attitudes of the rest of the world will bounce off the walls as though they were made of rubber and will not affect you.

---

The egg will stay with you afterwards for quite some time, but if you feel it has worn off, simply repeat the exercise. I have been using the egg and teaching people this exercise for years – since I read something similar in one of Betty Shine's books – and it is one of the most effective exercises in the repertoire. People who work with the public find it particularly useful as it takes away the immediacy of the offensive attitudes they encounter in some of the people they meet.

During my time as a computer teacher, for example, I once walked into a classroom and was met immediately by a student who seemed intent on interrogating me: was I using the very latest software?; did I know what I was doing?; how long was our lunch break? and so on. I could feel her questions hitting me like blows, so I pretended to hear a phone ringing outside, and quickly left the room. Once outside, I jumped into my egg and returned. The student continued her barrage but I didn't feel a thing! I was serene inside my egg and she couldn't ruffle me whatever she said. In fact, once she had settled down, she turned out to be a really good student.

We sometimes protect our aura automatically without realising why. Have you noticed that whenever you step into a lift and there is another person in there already, you automatically move to the furthest point of the lift? You are following a norm of our society, which is to respect other people's space. This space is a person's aura. It is considered rude and intrusive to move too close to another person when it isn't necessary.

If someone you didn't know were to stand right next to you, then you would most likely feel threatened. If, on the other hand, someone you loved moved into your aura you would feel happy. This is because their vibrations are recognisable to you, and they are probably on the same wavelength so you will be attracted to them. Vibrations and wavelengths are both descriptions of energy and, as I have said before, we use these terms every day to describe what we know subconsciously but don't see.

Whenever I travel, especially on long-distance plane journeys, I get into my egg. In planes and trains we are in close proximity to all sorts of people, and I am sure the reason we feel tired at the end of a plane journey is because of the number of people that surround us while we travel. We don't know what they are thinking and what state they are in.

The egg harms no one and it keeps you isolated from the thought forms of those around you. Hospitals are also places where you can feel your energies being sucked away from you. I am often visiting people who need help and I am very happy to give my time and love to those I see, but to keep strong while I'm there I find it best to put myself in my egg.

## Using the pyramid

While the egg is excellent for everyday use, there may be times when you need more protection: when you know that people are deliberately sending you bad vibes, for example (the expression is apt – their thoughts are vibrations of energy). Maybe you have upset someone; maybe someone is jealous of you – whatever the cause, the pyramid will help you keep their thoughts at bay. Follow the egg exercise but this time imagine a golden pyramid in front of you. Step into it. The pyramid will protect you from all offensive thought forms.

## The cloak and the flame

If you are ever faced with potentially dangerous circumstances – like walking through dark and gloomy streets or inner-city car parks at night, it will help you to feel less threatened if you have a psychic protection.

Visualise yourself surrounded with light and imagine that you are wearing a protective cloak of shining silver that makes you invisible. Another excellent protection is the violet flame – an ancient form of protection and one that I use when healing as it protects me from the negative energies of the person I am helping. To feel its protection, imagine yourself completely surrounded by purple flames.

## The games people play

We are constantly playing power games in our homes, whether we realise it or not. Every time you shout at a member of your family you are stealing their energy. The normal response, of course, is for that person to shout back at you to regain their power. Arguments are usually completely fruitless on account of this tit-for-tat exchange.

I want you to be aware that whenever you raise your voice or slam a door, you are taking energy from the person you are attacking. As their energy is taken, they will feel a dull pain in their solar plexus. At the time of the argument, this knowledge might give you some satisfaction. However, it is inevitably short-lived and arguments are very tiring. A house full of love is far more invigorating than one that is full of arguments and anger. Any buzz you may get from a shouting match fades very quickly.

Another technique, used mainly by women (sorry, ladies, but it does seem to be this way), is silence – the sulky 'I'm going to my room, so there' routine. It's a method of energy theft that my stepdaughter worked to perfection in her teens! As with verbal arguments, the person on the receiving end of this feels a pain in the solar plexus. Other games that we like to play are 'let's make you feel guilty' and 'I'm a victim/child'. They are both struggles for power and energy.

## Helping Yourself to More Energy

If you have followed the exercises so far, you now know how you can better handle your own and other people's emotional outbursts, and how to protect your energy. Let's look at a short breathing exercise that will give you a good boost and bring you into the state of love and peace.

---

EXERCISE: RAISE YOUR ENERGY
- Find a quiet place, close your eyes and relax.
- Imagine you have a tube running through the middle of you, from the centre of your head all the way down.
- As you breathe in, imagine that you are breathing white light down into the tube.

- Hold your breath for a moment and feel yourself in the state of love. To help yourself get into this state, think of someone or something you care deeply about, or think of something that makes you smile.
- As you breathe out, see the white light filling your aura.
- Continue breathing in and out for a few moments — be careful not to breathe too deeply, or you will begin to feel spaced out.

---

## What Are We?

You now know that we consist of more than just the physical body. We have looked in detail at our energy body and seen how it functions. However, we are even more than this! There are other aspects of our essence that are unseen and untouchable but that also have a huge role to play in our happiness and health. Our existence is made up not only of an energy body, but a mental and an emotional body as well. We shall be looking at our emotions and their effect on our health and wellbeing later on in the book.

Another, most important, unseen but vital element of our life form is our soul — our higher self, our greater being, our higher consciousness, that part of our being that is eternal, that moves on continuously in a cycle of birth and death. As we progress along our cyclical path, we grow and evolve spiritually. Everything that happens to us affects our soul, and much of the suffering and pain that we go through is our soul using our physical, mental and emotional bodies to heal itself.

As you continue through the book and along our path

of healing, you will start to feel good. This is the beginning of the inner happiness that comes only when your
soul is at ease. I shall be describing the working of the
soul and the cycle of life in more detail in chapter eight.
In the meantime, hold in your mind the knowledge that
every moment spent on improving your physical, mental
and emotional states assists the healing of your soul, the
very highest level of your being.

Let us now move on to look at how we can develop a
positive attitude and to consider the benefits of being
completely honest with ourselves and others.

# 2

# Honesty and Positive Thinking

Do you subjugate your true feelings? Do you even know what your true feelings are? In this chapter, we look at ways to get in touch with our emotions and so make choices that are based on personal truth. We consider why we lie and the harm it does. We learn to develop boundaries and the power of the word NO. Is your glass half-empty or half-full? We look at ways to think positively.

As we pass along our path of healing we shall be looking more closely at our loves, partners and relationships. Let's start by realising that it is possible to live life on our own terms and be honest about what we want and also to have healthy relationships.

## *The Truth*

Spiritual teachers have always taught that lying is wrong. There are two aspects of lying that I would like to consider here. The first is how our relationships with others are affected when we lie; the second is the effect avoiding the truth has on ourselves. However, we should begin by taking a closer look at what truth is.

When I was a child I had a very clear view of what was right and what was wrong. My ideas came down loud and strong from my parents. They told me that it was wrong to steal, to fight, to talk with my mouth full, to scribble on the walls, etc. In my world, right was always right and wrong was always wrong, and I was lucky enough to have parents who agreed on what was acceptable behaviour. It made my life very easy and straightforward.

The advantage of rules is that it makes it easier to make choices. I had a happy ride as long as I followed the rules and, because they were consistent, I could easily discern right from wrong myself. Not every child has these clear boundaries and those that don't have a confused impression of right and wrong from an early age – one minute they find a mode of behaviour is accepted and applauded, and the next minute they find themselves punished for doing the same thing. This is very often because parents themselves change their minds from moment to moment. They might hold a view strongly when they are energised and alert, but let things go by when they are tired.

## Deciding for ourselves

We are surrounded by rules and regulations throughout our lives, but as we get older we have the choice of following these edicts or making our own decisions about

what is right and wrong. If we decide to go against
society's rules then we will most likely be punished –
most of us decide that it is easier to go with the flow.
However, it's important to remember that this is exactly
what the people of Germany did under Hitler's rule.
They went with the flow of the time, although I'm sure
many of them were deeply disturbed by the rules that
they were following.

There are many modern political regimes that create
rules for their people which would be disputed if the
punishments for doing so were not severe. Even in a
democracy we still have to go with the majority, so we
are used to being restrained and dominated by other
people's ideas of what is right and wrong.

Some societies are less overpowering than others and
expect people to do as they are told to a lesser degree.
The French, for example, are notorious for disregarding
rules – I see this whenever we visit France and my
husband wants to smoke in a restaurant. Despite EEC
rulings he has never once been refused! The British might
argue the rules to the nth degree, but we tend to follow
them quite well once they are in place. In schools, the
amount of freethinking that is encouraged in children
varies from culture to culture. In China, children are
taught to obey and listen and not to ask too many questions, whereas American children are encouraged to have
their own opinions. This free-speaking system enables
people to find their own values and also their own truth
– what it is that resonates well with them. If you have
never been asked your opinion on a subject how can you
possibly decide for yourself what feels right?

## Relying on spiritual truths

From a spiritual perspective, I believe we should look for our own truths. We can seek guidance from teachers, governments, parents and friends, but at the end of the day we should learn to connect with our own inner truth. People often say to me that they just don't know what to believe, and guidelines can be useful – so I shall share my beliefs with you here, as I have been doing already. It can be difficult to distinguish the difference between the real truth and that with which we have been indoctrinated so I try to rely on spiritual truths as the basis for my own personal belief system. Here are some of them:

- What you give out, you get back – the law of cause and effect.
- There is a reason for everything that happens to us – there are no coincidences.
- Love is the foundation of all happiness.
- Fear is an obstacle that lies in the way of progress.
- We are all seeking a state of inner peace.
- We are all connected – the same energy flows between all living things.
- We should treat all living things with unconditional love and compassion.
- There are many, many routes to our personal nirvana and connection with God.
- It is wrong to harm any living thing gratuitously.

Of course, there are many, many more spiritual truths, but these are just a few that I rely upon to inform my decisions and use as an ethos for living. They don't always give me the whole answer – if I am deciding, for example, which house to buy or which dress suits me best then I have to trust in my own inner feelings. I know several people who find this kind of decision difficult because they have never had to stand alone and choose things for themselves. Do you find it difficult to make decisions even on a mundane level?

## Differences in perspective

The truth that I am going to ask you to connect with when you are making decisions in your everyday life will, of course, vary from person to person. These truths are borne from your personal perspective. In fact, I believe that all truth is ultimately a perspective. What will seem right to one person will seem wrong to another.

I have learned that the black and white world of my childhood is really a world of shades of grey. We each see things differently depending on our expectations and experience. I shall use the example of my husband to emphasise this. His first wife thought that he was a difficult man – she fell out of love with him and saw only his bad points or the things that she couldn't tolerate. When I met him, I saw a loving, generous man with a great soul and great humanity. I know he has some annoying habits (these will be left unstated for the benefit of us all!) but I see the total package that is him. It's a case of two women seeing the same man from totally different perspectives. What may be the right choice for you may be wrong for another, so try not to influence others too much with your point of view. Many wars have resulted from people and nations seeing the same situation from a different perspective and attempting to force the other side to their point of view.

## *Making Choices*

In order to be able to make choices for ourselves we need to get in touch with our intuition and our emotions. It's our emotions that tell us if we are happy or not. If we have lost touch with these measuring devices, we will have a hard time making choices because we won't be able to feel the surges of pleasure or repulsion that let us know whether or not something is good for us.

You might be out of touch with your feelings because you have been through some traumatic experiences in your earlier life, and have found that by putting up barriers between yourself and others you can avoid the close personal connections that can lead to emotional interdependency. You know that once you allow yourself to become involved emotionally with someone you will be vulnerable to being hurt.

We will be talking in depth about letting go submerged emotions – some people have locked their feelings away to such an extent that they cannot even feel the pain of the past, let alone consider letting it go. Such people cannot live their lives to the fullest as, although they feel no emotional pain, they also feel no joy. They are usually filled with fear or have low self-esteem, which stops them getting involved with their inner feelings and with others.

If this is your situation, I ask you to persevere: to continue to work through this book in its entirety and complete all the exercises. You should find that by the time you have finished and spent some time practising the ideas I have given you, you will be back in touch with your inner feelings and you will have healed many of your old wounds.

## Using your intuition

The reason I am emphasising the need for us to be in touch with our emotions is that the best way to make decisions and choices is through our feelings. It ensures that you are making a choice based on what feels right for you and not according to what your mind dictates, which has been indoctrinated with the rules and beliefs of others.

Through our inner feelings we connect with our intuition, which is directly connected to our soul and our higher self. This is the part of us that holds the wisdom and knowledge of our many lives and experiences. Since our intuition, or sixth sense, is connected to the very core of our being, it will guide us to where we need to be at all times. We shall look more closely at this in chapter eight, but for now I would simply ask you to bypass your mind when choosing what is right for you. You can further justify your choice with logic if that suits you, but your starting point should be your intuition.

Another thing I would like you to do is to be honest about your fears. They may well take you down a path that is not the best for you, so if you have any that could stand in your way then I suggest you look at them closely now. If you know what they are you are less likely to let them make your choices for you. If you were offered your ideal job, for example, but were frightened of taking it in case you failed, you would be being driven off your best course by fear.

If something makes you feel good and you truly want it, then do it. Don't be ruled by your fear. Fear is the obstacle that blocks our path forward.

## *Methods of Connecting to Your Inner Self*

Despite what I have said, you may still have a problem connecting to your inner self and knowing what is right for you. Here are some exercises and procedures that you can use that will help you bypass your mind and connect with your intuition. Some may work for you better than others – just keep your mind open.

The first exercise will help you identify the changes in your body when you are speaking the truth and when you are telling a lie. Our body acts as a barometer for our higher self and our innermost feelings. We have already discussed how it will get sick if we are out of balance or negative in our thinking. Our body will always confirm the state of our mind and emotions – it will let us know if we are happy or sad and it will respond to whatever is going on mentally, emotionally and spiritually. We can therefore make good use of it to help us understand whether we are telling ourselves the truth or not.

This exercise works on the basis that a lie makes us weak and the truth makes us strong. The more you practise, the easier you will find it to identify the messages your body is sending you.

---

EXERCISE: IDENTIFY YOUR PERSONAL TRUTH
- Find a quiet and peaceful spot where you will be undisturbed and free to concentrate on your body's responses.
- Close your eyes and breathe in deeply four times.
- Take a few minutes to let your concentration move around your entire body from your toes upwards.
- Now say a complete untruth out loud.

- Notice the feelings in your body – you may feel discomfort in your solar plexus; you may feel hot and uncomfortable (hot under the collar); you may feel your throat constricts a little as you speak so the words don't come out easily.
- Let your concentration move around your body again.
- Breathe in and out a couple times to clear the negative reaction.
- Now say something completely true – something that makes you happy.
- Feel your body's reaction – you may feel a soft warmth, a peaceful feeling. Remember this sensation. This is how your truth feels.

---

## The ring of truth

Before we leave the subject of the way our bodies respond to our thoughts, I should mention another sensation you may experience from time to time, when you say or think something that is spiritually true. The ring of truth feels like a tremor flowing through your body. It will often be concentrated around your neck and collarbone, or you may feel it rush through you and down your arms like an energetic vibration. I call it a 'whoosh' and it is a great indicator that I have made a positive statement of a spiritual nature. It acts as confirmation of a thought or insight.

## Kinesiology testing

If you still struggle to trust your 'personal lie detector' then you may find the following two processes helpful. The first procedure is taken from the science of kinesiology – the monitoring of the body via the muscles to connect with our higher self and show us what is best for our body and ourselves. Kinesiology can tell us whether we are short of any minerals or vitamins, and can be used to find the root cause of illnesses or mental and emotional problems. It is generally practised by alternative therapists like nutritionists and healers. My chiropractor also uses it, to help him diagnose his patients' problems.

EXERCISE: ASKING QUESTIONS USING THE
KINESIOLOGY MUSCLE RESPONSE TEST

In this example, I shall set out the process as used to test for food intolerance and sensitivities. You will need to ask a friend to help you.

- Remove any jewellery, watches, etc.
- Drink a large glass of water each – you need to be hydrated in order for the process to work properly.
- Make sure that neither of you is standing under a neon light or next to a microwave oven or television, as the micro and electromagnetic waves can affect results.
- Face each other and hold out your left arms.
- First test the process with a positive question: get your partner to ask you your name and answer them truthfully. Don't look into each other's eyes while you are doing this.
- Once you have given your truthful reply, your partner needs to push down your extended left arm with their right hand, exerting a reasonable pressure with their fingers. As you have told the truth, your partner will find it difficult to push your arm down. If you had lied, your arm would drop easily.

- Now you have tested the process, hold any substance or food you wish to check against your cheek with your right hand, and get your partner to check your muscle response in your left arm, as before. (You don't need to take anything out of its wrapping.) If you are intolerant to a food or have a sensitivity to it, your arm will drop easily.
- Use the process to see whether you need any vitamin or mineral supplements.
- Use the process whenever you want to know if something is beneficial for you – whether it's a physical thing, or something mental, emotional and/or spiritual.

## Making choices using a pendulum

In the first chapter I introduced you to the pendulum to help you check the state of your chakras. You can also use it as another method to help you make decisions about food, supplements and the source of your problems. In fact, the pendulum can help you make decisions and choices on any number of issues, by letting you know what is for your greatest good.

I like to visualise myself surrounded with light before using a pendulum. We open ourselves up and let our energy fields expand during the process so it's a good idea to protect yourself.

EXERCISE: ASKING QUESTIONS USING A PENDULUM
- Find a quiet space, and imagine yourself surrounded by white light.
- Hold your pendulum between the thumb and first finger of your strongest hand – the one you normally

use for writing. Let the chain of the pendulum hang down the back of your hand. Allow at least 15 cm of chain between your hand and the drop.

- Establish which way your pendulum will move when it has a positive 'yes' response by asking if your name is . . . (give your true name). Notice how the pendulum moves.

- Establish which way your pendulum will move when it has a negative 'no' response by asking if your name is . . . (give a false name). Notice how the pendulum moves.

- Now ask any question you want about yourself – always keeping to simple questions that require either a yes or no answer. Don't ask what vitamins you need, for example, but ask, 'Do I need any vitamins?' If the answer is yes, then ask, 'Do I need vitamin C?', etc.

- Alternatively, you can draw out a chart and let the pendulum select from various options. Hold the pendulum over the centre point of the chart and ask questions – for example, you may want to ask if you are sensitive to any of the foods which you have written/drawn on the chart.

---

Possible uses for your pendulum include:

- Checking whether you need any vitamins, minerals or supplements.
- Discovering what alternative medicines or healing processes would suit you.
- Finding out if you are sensitive or allergic to any foods – many people are sensitive to wheat and dairy products nowadays.
- Finding out which aromatherapy oils would help you.

- Selecting which book to read.
- Choosing a job.
- Finding things that you have lost (place a list of the likely places your lost item could be on a chart, then get the pendulum to show you).
- Uncovering the emotional or attitudinal problem behind a sickness – what thoughts and attitudes have created your physical illness. (We shall be looking at the association of thoughts and emotions with certain illnesses in chapter three.)

---

You can use the pendulum for many things but don't let it run your life for you. Always use it in combination with your own intuitive feelings.


## Speaking Out

We have been looking at the process of making decisions based on our inner needs, and how we can establish our own personal truth. Now I want to look at the effect avoiding the truth has on ourselves and others. Believe it or not, most of us tell lies all the time! We tell lies about our feelings, about what we really want to do or what we want from life.

We often tell lies because we say what we think other people want to hear rather than what we really mean. Do you ever do this? Do you work out what your partner or family want and then say what you think will please them? Or do you ever think that what you want will be laughed at and so keep your thoughts to yourself? Do you ever worry that what you would like to do will make someone else unhappy? This happens a lot in family situations – the mother who denies herself her own favourite food and cooks what her husband and children like instead; the woman who gives up a good job because she thinks she should spend more time at home; the man who would like to stay longer in bed in the morning but gets up because his wife is an early riser and expects him to be up too, pulling his weight with the household chores; the son that wants to go and live overseas but doesn't because it would upset his mother.

On a more everyday level, have you ever said you want the red wine because the bottle has been opened – and good manners seem to dictate that you go with the group choice – when you really want the white? Do you say what you like or want when you have the opportunity or do you prefer to let others choose for you? In all of these cases you are telling lies!

When you tell a lie or subjugate your own needs and wants, you will feel the effect – lies weaken you. Every time you tell a lie, whether it's an outright porker or a white one, and every time you keep quiet instead of speaking up – you damage your energy and your spirit. Remember the first exercise in this chapter, where you discovered how good and strong you feel when you tell the truth? The reverse applies when you deliberately keep quiet about your needs and feelings, whether this is in your relationships or at work.

Truth in the office can be difficult, I know. I worked for more than twenty-five years in the corporate business world and I was often pressurised into bending the truth. However, if you are constantly compromising yourself in the workplace, you ought to check whether the position you have really suits you. You may be better off looking for something that feels more comfortable and allows you to be yourself.

Let's think about why we often keep our feelings to ourselves. Do you suppress your wants and wishes because you don't want to upset other people in the family, or because you don't want to be judged by them? Are you fearful of what people will think or say? Or do you go along with the crowd because you want to be liked? These are just some of the reasons we lie. We often lie with the best of intentions and don't even realise that we are doing it because it has become a habit. But by denying the truth we are denying and belittling ourselves. We are feeding the 'I am unworthy' message that leads us to lose our self-respect and identity.

Consider the effect our lying has on others. How would you react if you knew that someone else always gave you priority? If you know that someone is always prepared to put your needs and desires first, it is all too easy to let them! From there we take the next step and start to take it for granted that we will always have our own way, and before long we get to the point where we feel angry and resentful if this doesn't happen. We can become a bully and totally dominate the other person. It isn't healthy for either party in a relationship if one person is always subjugating their own wishes in favour of the other person's.

## Establishing your boundaries

It is essential that you establish your personal boundaries. This means that you need to know how far you are prepared to go for another person. Be prepared to say no sometimes. You will be amazed how much others will respect you for speaking up and you will find that it makes group decisions much easier.

In my relationship with my husband, we have a system

where we both say what we would like and expect from situations – then we know where we are and, usually, we can find a way to accommodate the needs of both of us. In most families, arguments tend to arise over the smallest of issues, from which television programme to watch to whose turn it is to make tea. I am frequently shocked by how little give and take there is between some couples. I find that if I give in to my husband's wishes on one thing then he will succumb to my wants on another – we keep a balance that way.

## Saying no

You may need to say no sometimes when people ask for your time. I know several people who spend their lives running around after others. Of course, it's good to do things for people we love, but if this means that you are running from pillar to post and causing yourself stress, then dare to say no occasionally. Otherwise you will completely drain yourself of energy and be of no use to anyone. Keep some of your time for yourself.

I have a friend who is a healer and counsellor who used to be permanently attached to her mobile phone. Whenever we met, she would be speaking to someone else. I found it quite upsetting as it meant we couldn't complete a conversation without being interrupted by someone asking her advice. She was also always late for our appointments. Eventually I told her how upsetting this was. I explained that both myself and her other friends found it disturbing that she allowed herself to be taken away by her clients, no matter how needy they might be, when she was sharing our time. She had no boundaries in her life and couldn't say no to anyone.

Finally, my friend realised what was happening and

started to turn off the phone when she was having private time – which is a way of saying no. Now she is the most organised and punctual person I know. She has told me that the reason she gave so much of herself away was that she didn't have enough respect for herself – she thought other people were more important than herself. Do you do this? Do you think you are inferior to others?

---

**You are truly as good as anyone else and you have the right to be yourself, say what you think and also have time for yourself to do things that you enjoy, no matter what role you have in life.**

---

My mother was brought up in the days when women looked after their husbands and put them first in every respect. In fact, women were considered to be second-class citizens whose only real worth was as wife and mother. It was not surprising, then, that although my mother was (and is) a strong and powerful personality, she made my father's needs her first priority. Whatever she was doing during the day, she made sure that she was at home waiting for him and had a meal on the table as he walked through the door at 7 o'clock. His slippers were always ready by the fire and there was always a drink poured at his chair side. I can hear the men reading this applauding! However, my mother did all this to her own cost. She would never allow herself the pleasure of a day of freedom – one where she could come and go as she pleased without having to watch the clock and keep to a schedule. She ran her life entirely according to my father's timetable.

When I was in my teens my mother took a job in the

city and found great fulfilment in this. But when my father's work schedule changed and he had to work some Saturdays and have every other Monday off, she began to feel guilty. My father was a wonderful and loving man but he didn't enjoy his own company, and she worried when he had to spend the day alone. The stress she felt eventually became intolerable so, after a few months, she gave up her job so that she could be with him. It is full credit to her that she didn't show her resentment, but she certainly felt that her life was curtailed and diminished by her own attitude. The way she puts it is that 'she created a rod for her own back'. Because she had always given in and put her demands last, she was eventually expected to. My father had no consideration of the fact that she had given up a job that she really enjoyed – not because he was selfish, but because he expected her to be with him just as she always had been.

When my father died, my mother mourned deeply, but she also found the freedom to become her own person again. She can now voice her own opinions fully and confidently and I have seen a new woman stepping forth – one that has self-respect and an inner strength and happiness that I would never have thought possible given how close she was to my father. Her advice to younger women is to give, but not to give all of yourself away, to share but to keep something back for yourself.

## Be kind with your truth

You may think from what I have said that I condone a way of life that is self-centred and focused on one's own needs over and above the needs of others. This is far from the truth. I believe that one of the straightest paths to happiness is one that includes helping others. In my own life I allocate a great deal of time to healing and helping others to heal themselves. However, I also see the need to keep space for oneself and not to lose one's identity in the pursuit of aiding humankind. Likewise, it is essential that while speaking up for ourselves, we also spare the thoughts and feelings of others.

There are always two ways to do things and I advocate the way that causes the least amount of hurt to those involved. So when you want to tell your partner that you find his or her behaviour distressing, say it calmly and pleasantly and always add a smile if possible. If you need to speak up at work, be tactful and consider the feelings of your employer and colleagues. I know I hate to be bullied or spoken to angrily or arrogantly, so I suggest that even when you feel strongly about something you say what is on your mind as kindly as you can.

This is a story about someone I shall call Jane. Jane lived with Peter and they were happy together. Their characters were very different and they worked in totally different spheres. He worked in the corporate world and she was an aromatherapist so their values tended to be different too: he was keen to make money and progress in his career, while she had a more laid-back approach to life. However, they shared a love of adventure and sport and they had fun on their weekends.

Jane and Peter would argue from time to time over procedure and tidiness and correct behaviour, as you would expect a precise character and a laid-back character would, but they had lived together for several years. He always said he wanted to get married and have children and she – well, she kept quiet. Jane didn't want to make waves. She enjoyed her life with Peter and was quite happy to let it continue, but she didn't want children and she certainly didn't see herself with Peter for the rest of her life. She didn't say this to him because she was afraid he would break off their partnership. She was also aware that she was well supported, and aromatherapy doesn't pay too well.

Jane is a lovely person but if you had said to her that she was living a lie she would not have understood. However, one day Peter was offered a great job and he turned it down – because it would mean moving to a country where Jane would not be able to continue her work. She found out too late, when the opportunity had gone. Only then did she realise what she was doing to Peter.

Peter was living in the expectation of her spending the rest of her life with him. He had made a great sacrifice for her. Not only was she living in denial, she also felt guilty. She decided that she must speak her truth and she told him exactly how she felt. That was a very important day for her. She made both of them free spirits the moment she spoke up. Peter was able to reassess his relationship and, as it turned out, was quite accepting of her feelings about their partnership. The last I heard of them they were still together.

Once you start habitually speaking the truth and speaking up about your needs you will find that changes occur in your life. You will encourage honesty in your dealings with others and you will find that all your relationships improve. You will be treated with more respect and you will gain self-esteem.

Now that we know how we can get in touch with our feelings and know what we want from life, let's look at ways that we can change things and begin to see life in a more positive light.

## Creating a Positive Mind-set – Say it How You Want it to Be

I shall be showing you many ways in this book of how to look on the bright side of life, how to release emotional blocks and to see the good in all. Right now I'm going to address the problem of worrying, or having a cup that is half-empty instead of half-full.

---

EXERCISE: HOW POSITIVE ARE YOU?
We often slip into the habit, frequently picked up from our family or peers, of using negative words in our speech. Use this exercise to determine how often you use a negative word and see if you can begin to adopt more upbeat and positive words in future.

- Think about what words you use to describe your life. Do you cope, survive, struggle, manage, get by?
- How do you describe your job? Is it OK, draining, demanding, tiring or boring?
- How do you describe your country? Is it cold, wet, boring, OK?
- What about your partner? Is he or she miserable, demanding, OK?
- Start trying to use positive words from now on – let's enthuse about life! Try words like 'succeed', 'thrive', 'achieve', 'enjoy', etc. Take 'OK' and say 'wonderful' instead. Instead of 'I'll try', say 'I will'. Don't say 'all right', say 'fantastic'.

---

I'd like you to start listening to yourself in general. Watch out for any signs of negativity in your conversations and the things you say either to yourself or to others. The spoken word is powerful – as we say things we are committing them to fact. If we continually say 'I'm unlucky', we are creating an unlucky thought form that will sit in our aura and, guess what, make us unlucky!

> During our time in Malaysia, my husband and I booked a table at the Australian Ball with a number of our friends. The big event of the night was the prize draw. As we sat down for dinner, all I could hear around me was 'I never win draws', 'I've never won anything in my life', 'This'll be a waste of time', and so on. I said, 'I'm always lucky' – and it's true. My close friend also has a strong positive streak and she said that she, too, often won prizes. So when the numbers were announced it was no real surprise to me that I won the first prize of two return tickets to Sydney and my friend won third prize. In fact, she did *very* well as I took her with me to Oz and we had a wonderful holiday!

Every time we say something negative we are brain-washing ourselves into that state. Listen out for the following types of comment, and ask your friends and family to help you by telling you whenever they hear you being negative. It might make them think about whether they have this habit too!

- My boss doesn't like me.
- I always get colds at this time of year.
- I always get sick on my holidays.
- I never win lotteries or raffles.
- I'm useless at exams.
- I can't . . .

- I'm no good.
- I'm fed up.
- I'm bored.
- I'm always late, etc., etc.

## Using affirmations

If you discover that your conversations are peppered with negative expressions, don't despair – help is on the way. It is possible to turn yourself around and it's surprisingly simple. You need to introduce positive affirmations into your life. An affirmation is a statement of how you want things to be. You can brainwash your mind at a conscious and subconscious level into new thinking patterns. You can fill your aura with positive energy with the words you use.

I have used this technique to help with weight loss, to calm myself down in tense situations and to give myself confidence when I have felt nervous. Louise Hay, the famous author of many inspirational books, used affirmations to recover her health when diagnosed with terminal cancer.

You can do anything you wish and you can be anything you wish. It's up to you.

---

EXERCISE: USING POSITIVE AFFIRMATIONS
- Sit down and quietly relax for a few minutes. Think of the things you want in your life and the attitudes you would like to change.
- Look through your list and pick your two highest priorities.
- Write an affirmation that will bring these into your life. For example:

- If you are forgetful: 'I am focused and clear and I have a good memory'.
- If you never have any money: 'I bring abundance into my life'.
- If you are depressed: 'My life is full of light and my spirits rise moment by moment'.
- If you are bored: 'My life is full of interest and I actively attract fun and stimulation'.

• Be careful how you word your affirmations:
  - Only use positive words: say, 'I am upbeat and happy' rather than 'I *never* get depressed'; 'I prefer savoury food' rather than 'I *don't* like sugar'.
  - Avoid the words *want, wish* or *need*, as you will create the state of being wanting, wishing or needy.
  - Make sure you truly want to attract the situation you state – winning the lottery may sound great, but it could ruin your life. Choose instead to call abundance into your life.

• Say your affirmations out loud every day and as often as possible, and visualise the words of your affirmations. It might take a while or the changes might be instantaneous, but it will always work.

• If your affirmations are very emphatic – 'I am happy at all times', for example – you may be being too hard on yourself. It isn't realistic to expect to be happy all the time so such a bold affirmation needs a shadow that says, 'but it's OK to be down a little at times'. This will allow you to be a little gentler on yourself and will stop you from feeling guilty if you don't measure up.

---

Now is a good time to take a quick look at the list of attitudes and thought patterns that you wrote down earlier.

Do you see now how you can change some of these? Do you see how they are making you unwell? There is much more to come – just remember that it will take a while to make a complete turn around but if you have the intention to change then, without doubt, you will. A positive attitude and a smile will take you a long way.

---

Every smile, every kind word, every thoughtful act will have an effect – not only on others but also on yourself.

---

## The Effect of Our Actions

We have looked at the ways in which our thoughts and words can affect our health and we are now going to look at the effect of our actions. I truly believe that there are no accidents and that everything happens for a reason. This belief has helped me through a tremendous number of what could be described as traumatic events in my life.

As our thoughts are energetic messages that create either light or darkness in our auras and those of others, so our actions also bring light or darkness and have an effect on our energy field and the energies of those around us. In its natural state, this world is full of harmony and balance, and as energetic beings with choice and free will we can choose to go with the harmony of life or go against it.

I think of the analogy of the surfer who can reach the beach from far out to sea if he catches the big wave – by letting nature take him, he can travel all the way – by going with the flow. If the surfer were to fight nature he would end up swimming to the beach and being buffeted and bounced by the waves instead of being gently taken in by them. Life is like the sea and the trick is to get with the flow.

Later on in the book, I shall suggest some ways in which you can connect with the flow of life, but now I want to look at how our actions affect the ebb and flow of life around us.

## We are all connected

I have talked at length about the energy that flows through and around us. The source of this energy is the life force that serves all mankind. It is often referred to as Universal Energy. This energy of spirit flows through every living thing – so we are all connected. If we harm or upset any being, we harm and upset the total consciousness, the total life force of all humanity and all that lives. This connection is called group consciousness and it affects us all.

This is a true story about a group of Japanese anthropologists who were studying the behaviour patterns of monkeys. They worked on an archipelago and each man was based on a separate island. One man noticed that the monkeys in his control group were picking up fruits from the beach and spitting out the sand that covered them. He wondered if they could learn a new way, so he began picking up the fruits himself and washing them in the sea.

The monkeys watched him and then copied him, happily eating clean fruits. However, it wasn't only the monkeys on this island that took up the new way of eating their fruits – all the other monkeys on the other islands did too! They were out of sight and out of hearing distance, but they had picked up the habit from the thought form of the total group – once enough monkeys had learned the new way then all the monkeys knew it. This is group consciousness at work.

We can surmise from this example that if enough people in the world are kind and giving and in the state of love, then all humanity will be affected. Food for thought.

If you deliberately cause a person or animal hurt the universe has to respond. At some stage in your life you will be affected by your actions. Looking on the positive side, this means that if you deliberately do something to help someone you will get the benefit returned to you – in one way or another. So another excellent way to move towards a happier, more fulfilling and positive life is to take time out to help others in any way you can.

Watch out for people to help – it's amazing what you can do just on your way to work if you are looking. It is often concern about what other people will think that holds one back from stepping into the limelight, but in my experience it's not the things that we do for people that disturb us afterwards but the things we didn't do. It's the puppy obviously lost at the side of the road that we don't go back and pick up that haunts us for years, not the one we rescued and took back to its owner.

I am speaking from my heart here – and I have learned my lessons as we all have – but I hope now that whenever I see something that pulls at my heart strings, I will respond without thinking. Once we begin to think, our mind steps in and logic comes on at a gallop to talk us out of our natural inclinations.

Regrets are kind thoughts that we didn't put into action.

## *Asking the Universe for Help*

Before we leave this chapter on truth, choices and the power of thinking positively, I would like to give you a way to help yourself if you are worrying over something in your life. Worry is disruptive and gets us nowhere but it is sometimes difficult to avoid, especially when we have important decisions to make. So why not ask the universe for some help next time? When I want confirmation about a plan or an idea I ask for three confirmations and I always get them if I'm on the right track. Confirmations can come from a book you happen to pick up, an article in a magazine you just happen to glance at, or a friend may ring you and say something that will act as a sign. Keep your eyes, mind and ears open and you will see the indications. Do this today. Ask the universe to give you some confirmation about anything that is troubling you and see what happens.

# 3

# Emotions and Their Effects

In this chapter we see how emotions and thoughts – whether our own or other people's – can affect our well-being and our health. We consider how the attitudes of our parents and culture can influence us, and look at ways to let go emotional baggage and review our experiences positively. We look at two of the most difficult emotions, anger and fear, and find ways to deal with them.

Our emotions and thoughts have deep and often lasting effects on our state of mind and, ultimately, on our health. Negative emotions and thoughts transmit themselves as negative energy. If we can turn ourselves around and rid ourselves of negativity, we will be able to heal ourselves and others with our positive vibrations.

## *Emotions, Thoughts and Our Aura*

### Emotions

I mentioned earlier that a healthy aura is normally egg shaped, but our thoughts and emotions, and the onslaught of other people's thoughts and emotions, can affect its shape, form and position.

Although most of us are unaware of these constant changes on a conscious level, we pick up all sorts of messages from other people's auras unconsciously. In fact, we often comment on what we see through our verbal descriptions of a person's state. We use expressions like:

- 'Who's ruffled your feathers?' – to describe the porcupine look of an agitated or prickly aura.
- 'All over the place' – to describe an unfocused and scatty person, whose aura has been pushed beyond its normal boundaries by scattered feelings or thoughts.
- 'Beside himself' – to describe an aura that is totally off balance and has been thrown to one side as a result of shock or severe agitation.
- 'I felt as though I had been punched in the stomach' – to describe the state of the aura following a shock, which can literally have the appearance of being punched.

So although we may not see the effects of emotions on our aura, our sixth sense will pass the message to our brain and we will verbalise what we sense. The aura literally changes shape to reflect what we are feeling. A person who is depressed will have an aura that is grey and comes in down close to their body. Someone who is full of life and bounce will have a bright and shining aura. If we start clinging to another person our energy field will create hooks to attach ourselves to that person as we drain them of their energy – this is where the expression 'getting their hooks into you' comes from. A hysterical person will have an aura that shoots off in many directions and a person who is deflated and down will have an aura that reflects exactly this.

### The Effects of Different Emotions on the Aura

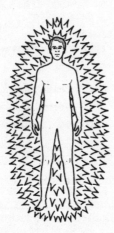

Irritable
and tetchy

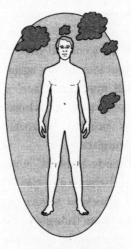

Aura with negative
thought forms
creating blocks

*A healthy aura is usually egg shaped (see opposite, top and bottom right), but different emotions can affect this shape, as shown on this and the following two pages.*

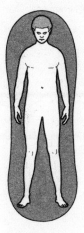

**Depressed**
'Low' – dark

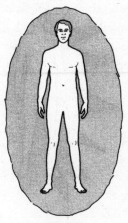

**Happy**
Outgoing and light

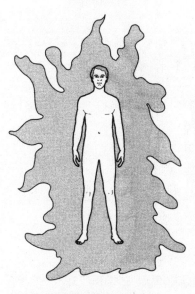

**'All over the place'**
unfocused mind – dissipates
and weakens energy

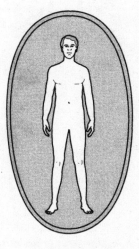

**Strong boundries**

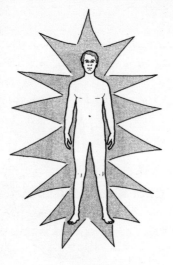

**Angry**
Each thought sends
out a 'spear' of energy

**Shocked**
A punch to
the stomach

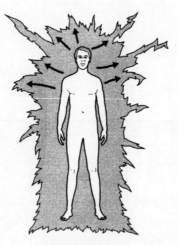

Hysterical

## Thoughts

Our thoughts and the thoughts of others can also affect the state of our aura. Every thought we have has an effect on either ourselves or another person. This is because *every thought is a beam of energy*. This is an extremely important message and is the key to the reason why our attitudes affect our health.

At the moment a thought is formulated in your mind it becomes an energetic force. The energy of this thought will then attach itself to the object of the thought. If you are thinking about yourself, the energy will attach itself to your aura – your energy field. If you are thinking of someone else, this stream of your energy will attach itself to that person's energy field, no matter where they are. Distance makes no difference to the power of the energy sent.

My organisation Hearts and Hands (*see page 260*) has a healing network through which we send healing to people in this way all around the world. Think of your personal energy source as a reservoir and our thoughts like a stream. As we think of someone kindly so we create a life-giving stream of energy that will flow directly into their reservoir.

Let me tell you a little about the difference between positive and negative thoughts. Although I use the word 'negative', there is actually no such thing as a wrong thought – every thought is an experience and our lives are filled with experiences that give us opportunities to grow. However, for the purposes of this definition I shall use the word negative to mean dark, downcast, miserable and disempowering, and positive to mean uplifting, empowering, bright and light.

When we think of something uplifting the energy flow

we create is strong and powerful and it will increase the power and strength of the pool of energy it joins. For example, if I send thoughts of love to my friend who is suffering depression because he has lost his job, my thoughts will help him by increasing his energy flow and making him feel brighter.

If I were to send thoughts of him suffering and see pictures in my mind of him getting more and more depressed and losing his home and family, then the energy I was sending would only make him feel worse. This is why worrying about someone is the very last thing we should do as, rather than helping, we are causing further distress. (I shall be explaining ways that we can use this energy of thought for the benefit of others later in the book.)

As every thought produces a reaction at the point of its focus, we can affect our own state of mind instantly with our thoughts. My local health club instructor told me that if an athlete has a negative thought it takes just four seconds for it to affect his performance. Let's see how our thoughts affect us in this next exercise.

---

EXERCISE: FEEL THE EFFECTS OF YOUR THOUGHTS
Follow these visualisations and note the effects they have upon you. If you can't see these pictures in your mind, don't worry, just think about them and sense the situation.

• Find a quiet place and close your eyes.
• Imagine you are sitting in a dentist's chair.
• Watch the dentist as he leans over you with a fiendish grin and a drill in his hand.
• He gets closer and closer.
• Now open your eyes. How do you feel? Not good, I'm sure.

Next try the following:

- Close your eyes and breathe deeply four times.
- Imagine that it is a beautiful sunny day. There is a slight breeze and it is keeping you at a perfect temperature.
- You are walking along a path towards an old red brick wall that surrounds your private garden.
- You see a gate in the wall – open the gate and step inside to the garden of your dreams.
- See your favourite flowers, see flowering bushes and trees.
- Wander along the paths that meander through this perfect place, this sanctuary of tranquillity and peace.
- Can you sense the peace? Can you smell the fragrances of the flowers? Can you hear the birds singing?
- See a pond with a fountain at its centre. Sit and dangle your fingers in the water.
- Take time to enjoy the serenity of the beauty that surrounds you.
- When you feel ready, slowly go back through the gate – looking around your garden one more time. Know that you can return whenever you wish.
- Walk back down the path into the room.

You should feel a great deal more relaxed after thinking about the garden than you did with the dentist. Note how you feel – are you calmer, more relaxed? Do you feel warm and good inside? If so, well done, you achieved this yourself using your thoughts and your imagination.

## The Effects of Thought Forms

Of course, one-off thoughts like those described above will only have a short-term effect. But if you were to have the same thoughts over and over again, as you do when you worry, then the effects will be more lasting.

When we consistently think negative thoughts the energy of these thoughts will collect together: similar energies attract each other and collude to create a miasma of energy called a thought form. Visually, it resembles a tangle of threads, a heavy congestion. Although I rarely see these thought forms, I can feel them when I'm passing my hands through someone's aura during healing and they have a sticky, thick quality.

A thought form that is not dispelled will eventually stop the natural flow of the auric field and block the flow of the meridians. Acupuncturists and reflexologists also aim to unblock the meridians, by using needles or finger pressure on specific pressure points on the body or feet to send energy through and clear the pathways.

You may wonder how these thought forms affect you on a day-to-day basis. Well, the most obvious and commonly experienced outcome is a headache. Most people have experienced stress – a form of worry where you have the same thoughts churning over and over in your head consistently.

Stress can be due to a variety of reasons. Maybe you are under pressure to complete a project and you fear that you will fail to meet a deadline, or you are frightened your baby will catch a disease, or you are fearful of losing your job, missing a plane, being late for an appointment, etc. The initial outcome will be the same – the thought form will build up in your aura and the energy will get blocked – and very often you will end up with a headache. I sometimes feel the thought form of a patient's headache like a heavy ball that is pressing down on their head.

The exercise I shall be introducing you to in a moment is ideal for clearing headaches but will also clean your aura and give you a feeling of peace and calm. You will be literally sweeping away the negative thoughts that have collected around your body. Whenever I get stressed I take myself to a quiet place and spend just a few moments calming and clearing myself. It works wonders.

## More energy healing – sweeping

This next process takes the energy healing process I showed you in chapter one a step further. So far we have used the healing symbol to invoke the energies that come through our hands to lift us and replenish our energetic resources. We have also used this energy stream to balance and heal our chakras.

Now we are going to look at the simple but effective clearing method of sweeping. It is a process I use before I perform any healing as it clears away the negative thought forms from the aura. These thought forms could be your own or other people's, which have attached them-selves to you. Whatever their source, you will feel lighter and calmer once they are removed.

---

EXERCISE: SWEEP AWAY NEGATIVE THOUGHT FORMS
This exercise is excellent for headaches or a muzzy head, and for releasing depressive thoughts. It will calm you down, so do it whenever you feel hyper or nervous. I use it just before I have to stand up and speak in public.

- Using your fingers as combs, sweep through your aura from the top of your head down to your feet.

- Sweep down your arms and down your body.
- Flick the negative energy away to somewhere safe –
  not in your cat's face or at plants, or your friends, family
  or passers-by! A bowl of salty water will help as salt
  attracts and absorbs negative energies (hence the reason
  we feel so light and uplifted after a trip to the sea).
  Just flick your hands at the water after each sweep.
- If you are doing a thorough sweep, continue the
  process for about five minutes. But you can do mini
  sweeps any time of the day, whenever you need to
  calm down.

---

Try the following visualisation either after sweeping or
as a separate exercise.

---

EXERCISE: CLEAR YOUR ENERGY FIELD OF NEGATIVE
THOUGHT FORMS

Since I learned this technique, I have almost never had
to resort to painkillers for headaches. Try it as soon as
you feel a headache coming on. Or you can use it after a
day's work, either on the train or when stuck in a traffic
jam!

- Breathe in deeply four times – breathing deeply into
  your stomach.
- Imagine there is a white tornado dropping on to your
  head and spinning away all the negativity. Take your
  time. See the spinning, swirling light slowly, slowly
  moving down over your head.
- Watch the light moving down your body, slowly
  sweeping away all the thought forms in its path –
  yours and those of others that have attached themselves to you.

- See it pass down and slowly disappear into the ground beneath you, taking with it all the debris of the day.
- Sit quietly for a few moments afterwards and continue to breathe naturally but deeply.

---

## *Understanding Your Emotions and Your Thoughts*

At this point it would be a good idea for you to write down all your personal character traits, attitudes and dominant thoughts and emotions. Are you naturally happy-go-lucky, for example, or do you worry easily?

- Do you look on the bright side of life or are you pessimistic?
- Are you lucky or unlucky?
- Are you self-critical or happy with the way you are?
- Do you set yourself high goals that are not easily obtainable?
- Do you think that life has been kind or unkind to you so far?
- Do you have difficulty saying you are sorry?
- Do you often feel resentment or do you find it easy to forgive?
- Do you cry easily?
- Do you have any fears – if so, what are they?
- Do you let people push you around and dominate you?
- Do you continually find yourself in jobs or relationships that make you unhappy?

I shall be addressing many of the character traits and attitudes referred to in this list later on in the book – but firstly let's consider whether any of your thinking results from your culture or family background.

---

Our background is the platform of our character and the stage for our life's performance.

---

## The effects of our culture

I explained earlier that we can affect others with our thoughts, so it will be no surprise to learn that we are seriously affected by the thoughts and mind-sets of those around us. The attitudes of our culture and the country where we were raised combine in an extremely powerful thought form, which affects us from the moment we are born. You are therefore bound to find some of your cultural and national heritage in your thinking patterns. Many British people, for example, have the traditional 'stiff upper lip' and are loath to show their emotions in public.

Just take a moment or two to think about your own national and cultural background. Do you think you are affected by the mind-set of your culture? Have you developed behavioural and thinking patterns as a result of your religion or race? You can decide for yourself if this has been detrimental or advantageous for you. The important thing is that you realise these influences and can distinguish between your own personal preferences and the limitations of what has been placed on you.

Everything that happens to us will affect us for the rest of our lives.

## Family thought patterns

Some of your thought patterns will have been given to you by your family. Family thought patterns affect you because they are with you from birth. Look again at the list you made of your characteristics and check to see how many you may have picked up from your family. Take a good look at your mother and father and other relatives and see if you follow any family trends. Even if you don't take after them, you will have been affected by their thinking. If your parents were worriers, the stress will have affected you. If they argued a lot, you will have been affected by the negative energies in the home.

Studies show that there is a correlation between thinking patterns and illnesses. So what may seem like inherited illnesses may, in fact, be inherited mind-sets. Let me give you an example. Many healers have found that arthritis can be connected with being over-critical – usually of oneself – and of not letting go, not going with the flow of life.

In my family there seems to be an inherited tendency to arthritis on my mother's side: my grandfather, mother and uncle have all had osteoarthritis of the hip. Now I don't know about my grandfather, but I do know that my mother and uncle are very self-critical and set themselves high goals. They were also brought up by a demanding woman – a high achiever, to use the modern expression (yes, I'm talking about the same grandmother who introduced me to healing).

It is a recognised family trait that we like to take on a heavy workload and then look around for more. Sitting and relaxing and letting life take us on its flow has always been difficult for all of us – apart from my one uncle who didn't get arthritis! My husband has been a good influence on me because he has the knack of totally relaxing whenever he gets the opportunity. He has taught me that it's OK to sit and read a book or take a walk just for the sheer fun of it.

Before I met my husband I was also beginning to get all the symptoms of arthritis. I can remember on our first wedding anniversary struggling to climb hills and having deep cramping pain in my hip joint. Fortunately, the problem has now gone away and I believe this is due to two things. Firstly, I changed my eating habits, as I had read that the wrong diet can aggravate the condition and, secondly, I learned to relax. I healed myself, although without consciously realising it at the time.

If your family has an 'inherited' weakness, don't think that you have to have this problem yourself. Once you have acknowledged that your family's thought patterns can affect your health, you can ensure that you change your thinking. Remember to use affirmations and you will discover that these can have an amazing effect. In other words, watch your family and learn from their mistakes!

### *If you need further help*

These days there is counselling available for people who have been mistreated and abused as children. It really is a good idea to seek professional help if you are holding on to any memories that you cannot or don't wish to share with either your family or friends. It is important to let go these old memories and traumas, and counselling can help you release them and let you move on in your life.

Speak to your doctor and they will be able to give you the name of a local counsellor who can help you. You may also consider visiting a healer. If you don't wish to tell anyone about your problem but would still like to get some relief from the experience, a healer can be a good option. I often heal people of private issues without actually knowing the details of the problem, as a healer's role is to help clear away emotional and upsetting imprints left on the energy field by traumatic events of the past.

## Using Illness as an Indicator

I use the correlation between disease and attitudes as an indicator of the cause of a patient's illness. It is amazing how many times I can work backwards from the illness to the thinking or emotional disturbance and imbalance that is the root of the problem. (If you would like to study this subject in more detail I suggest you read the books written by Debbie Shapiro and Louise Hay – see Further Reading, *page 258*). Your body will always give you messages, letting you know whether it is happy or not with the way you are leading your life. The pains and physical problems we have are very often warnings and signs to look within. If we ignore these signs then we can expect more serious problems in the future. I believe that there is always a cause behind pain and disease, just as there is a reason for everything else in life.

### Why we get sick

There are many reasons why we get ill. You need to study your lifestyle, your working habits, your diet and how you handle your emotions – consider whether you care

for yourself enough, for instance. I have made a list of
some common ailments and illnesses and the mind-sets
that are often connected with them. Look through and
think about whether your physical problem is rooted in
a thought pattern.

I have suggested some self-healing exercises and
processes and, where appropriate, I have included healing
symbols that have been given to me to help with specific
problems. Use these symbols intuitively: if you feel they
will help with any of your problems try them out. They
have many uses and can help with a variety of situations.

Please use these notes as indications only – I am sharing
them with you as they may help you find a pattern of
thinking or attitude that sits behind your own problems.
I am not saying they are the absolute or only reason for
your sickness.

## Accidents

I believe that there is a reason for everything, so there
are no true accidents. One of the commonest reasons for
falls, for example, is that we have become out of balance
in our life. If we are taking on too much, are overwhelmed
or over-burdened, we cannot expect to stay up straight.

If you are involved in a car crash, think about whether
you needed this jolt to re-evaluate your life. Are you
rushing off in the wrong direction, or is your energy
being spread across too many projects or issues just now?
There will always be a message behind an 'accident' and
a reason to stop and think.

### TRAUMA SYMBOL

This symbol helps clear the pain and shock of injury. To
be most effective it should be administered as soon as the
event has occurred. If you bang your knee, for example,

draw the symbol immediately and then hold your hand on or above the injury. It will also minimise bruising.

*Draw the symbol in an anticlockwise direction, starting in the centre and working outwards. Finish by pointing your finger into the middle of the symbol. Draw the symbol three times.*

## AIDS

This disease, which affects the immune system and our defences, can be caused by denial and a retreat from the facts of our lives. If we are totally honest about our needs and desires we will be in harmony with our bodies. Disharmony, whether this is the result of being personally out of balance or due to the misalignment of global energies, harms us.

The enormous numbers of people affected by AIDS, and cancer, leads one to suspect that the disharmony of the world and the problems of toxic overload are taking their toll. Use the forgiveness exercises in chapter six for yourself and humanity, and let go any feelings of guilt.

A young AIDS sufferer I knew in Singapore became at peace with himself and his illness once he had admitted his homosexuality to his mother. Much of his mental distress and suffering had been caused by the guilt he felt at deceiving her. I also suggest working on self-esteem and inner worth and value. As with cancer, a healthy diet and detoxification can help the immune system.

## *Arthritis*

When we hold on too tightly to our thoughts and emotions, crystals can form around our joints and cause them to seize up. Alleviate the symptoms by being less critical of yourself and so letting your energy flow. Allow yourself to do some really silly things and be spontaneous. Take a look at the sections on self-esteem and love in chapter four, and try loving yourself a little better.

### SYMBOL FOR PAIN RELEASE

This symbol will help you let go all forms of pain.

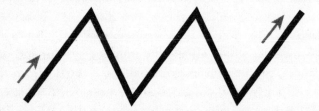

*Draw from left to right, starting at the point of pain and throwing the end as you release the pain energy from your hand. Repeat as many times as necessary.*

## *Asthma*

Asthma is a form of panic. It is often exacerbated by difficult family relationships and the overwhelming demands (loving or otherwise) of a close family member, often the sufferer's mother (smother mother syndrome). Help yourself by releasing the fear – see the exercises for letting go old emotions and fear later in this chapter. Avoid dairy products as they create mucus.

### Back pain (lower back)

Back pain is directly connected to issues of security, often financial. You may be lacking support in your family or workplace. Do you worry about the future? Are you worried that you will not be able to manage financially? If your back pain is an old, recurring problem, think about what you were thinking and fearing when you first developed it. Affirm to yourself that all your needs are and will be met – the universe will provide. It might sound trite but it's absolutely true.

I once looked out at two men working in my garden who were building a new wall as part of some alterations we were having done to our house. I saw the older man holding his back and wincing. Later that day I asked him if he had a back problem. He said he had and that it flared up from time to time. His young companion also complained that he had recently developed a problem in his lower back.

As I placed my hands on the young man's back, I asked him whether he was about to take on or had recently taken on a commitment – marriage or something similar. He jumped and looked at me. 'How did you know that?' he asked. 'My partner wants us to get married.' He was convinced that I was a witch!

In fact, it was easy for me to work out his problem as lower back pain is nearly always associated with security fears. He was worried about taking on the responsibility of a wife and his worry had manifested itself in his back. Once he recognised this, it didn't take more than a couple of minutes to shift the pain.

His older companion was also worrying about the future. His working life had always been somewhat hit and miss, and he was not getting work as regularly as a man of his age would like. You don't need to be psychic to work out the causes of most ailments – our bodies will tell us what the problem is.

### Back pain (shoulders and neck)

Most people suffer from back problems at some time in their lives. Nearly everyone I treat suffers from some discomfort in their upper back occasionally – anything from tension to severe pain. This is the area of the body where we hold responsibilities for others.

Worrying about your children or an overload of work responsibilities could be the cause of your neck and shoulder pain. (It is often referred pain – although your shoulder may hurt the root of the problem could be the vertebrae at the top of your spine.)

Try helping yourself by cutting the cords (see chapter five) between yourself and your responsibilities, on the basis that everyone is responsible only for themselves. Or if you have small children – who are indeed your responsibility – then I suggest you get regular massage, take time out for yourself if and when you can, and make sure you have a good-quality pillow. You will also find that regular meditation and/or yoga will help you relax.

### Boils and spots

A build-up of negative thoughts can erupt in boils and spots. They could also be caused by repressed anger. Maybe you have decided to let go your old thought forms and your body is mirroring this by letting go the toxins and poisons that have built up. Drink plenty of water to help flush out your system.

### Breaks and fractures

Have you been pushing yourself to the limit? Is your body at breaking point? You may need a rest – a broken arm or leg will make sure you get this chance to stop and slow down.

### SYMBOL FOR BREAKS AND FRACTURES

This symbol is used to heal breaks in bone, tendons, sinews or anything that has been fractured in any way.

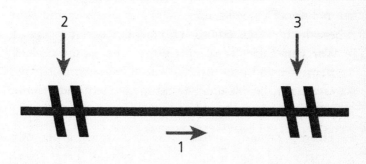

*Trace the above symbol from left to right over the damaged part of your body, keeping the two sets of vertical lines on either side of the break. Draw the two sets of vertical lines from top to bottom, starting at the left of the horizontal line as shown.*

### Cancer

A doctor I know, who runs a daily clinic for cancer patients, has told me that the main causes of cancer are toxicity, stress, nutritional deficiencies and radiation.

- **Toxicity** Our body's toxicity is caused by pollutants in our drinking water and the pesticides and unnatural additives we are exposed to in our food. We can also poison ourselves with alcohol, drugs and cigarettes. Detoxify yourself regularly to give your body a chance to get back into balance and fight the cancer. Many people have had great success by detoxifying themselves (drinking only fruit and vegetable juices) for a few days a month, and following a light organic diet the rest of the time, avoiding caffeine, red meat and dairy products. Eat plenty of broccoli as this is high in natural antioxidants – cancerous cells develop when there is a toxic overload. You can also be adding toxins to your system through the things you rub into and spray on your skin, so try to use hair and skin products using natural ingredients where possible. I also avoid the use of anti-perspirants as these block the pores and prevent the natural emission of toxins. Generally, be extremely kind to yourself and reserve your energies as best you can.

- **Stress** Constant anxiety, fear and worry lower our energy and deplete our immune system. Treat yourself well and take time for meditation, massages and quiet reflection. Manage your time – we often don't give ourselves enough room in our busy schedules. (See also the section on stress later in this chapter, and chapter four, where we discuss ways to treat ourselves a little better.)

- **Nutrional deficiencies** The vegetables that we eat are often lacking in vital vitamins and minerals due to the overworking of our fields. A good colloidal vitamin and mineral supplement can help to give us those essential elements that are missing from our food. Always buy organic products when you can.

- **Radiation** The air around us is filled with microwaves and electromagnetic pollution. Avoid these hidden dangers to our health by always turning off your TV (don't leave it on standby); not having a clock radio by your bed; avoiding unnecessary X-rays; not buying a new home near an electricity pylon or substation.

I can also recommend www.cancerhelpcentre.co.uk, an extremely helpful website for cancer sufferers. It is run by a medical doctor who specialises in identifying the causes of cancer, and is full of genuinely practical advice and alternative healing suggestions. Believe you can be healed – there are many, many stories of people treating themselves and achieving complete recovery. Visit the website and also read some of the wonderful books written by people who have conquered this disease, including Louise Hay and Matthew Manning (see Further Reading, *page 258*).

I am personally convinced that the toxins the global community has dispelled into our environment are responsible for the current 'plague' of cancer throughout the world. We suffer from a global lack of respect for our planet and its environment.

Although you personally may have a caring attitude towards the Earth and the environment, the universal law of cause and effect means that the actions of the whole world affect us all. Mankind generally has misused the Earth's resources, and pollution is rife. On both a physical and spiritual level we are being affected by the results of our actions. It is up to us to demand changes. We can shun non-organic food and protest where we can about the emission policies of our governments. We can do our bit to recycle and avoid products that cause pollution. And we can use the power of our thoughts and minds to heal our planet (see chapter eight for a planetary healing meditation that can help us redress the balance and heal our world).

### Candida

Are you a worrier? Candida is the physical symptom of a digestive tract that is out of balance. For the low energy symptoms, take a natural energy booster like Q10 Enzyme – I have found this excellent for boosting energy. Try Pau d'arco as a remedy for healing the digestive system. I also suggest you detoxify yourself as this will help you get your digestive tract back into balance.

### Chest infections

Any difficulty in breathing is related to fear or resentment. We hold our problems on our chest (hence the expression 'getting it off our chest'). So speak up and let people know what is bothering you – do it as kindly as you can, but speak up. I have seen many people released from their breathing restrictions by literally getting their problems off their chest in our sessions.

Fear inhibits our breathing and when we are fearful we tend to take shallow breaths. Use the fear release exercise at the end of this chapter and try some of the breathing exercises gently to encourage your lungs to breathe a little deeper and take in more oxygen.

If you have a chest infection, take a piece of ginger, grate it, boil it and drink the tea. Another natural remedy, which I came across in the Far East, is Tiger balm, which can be rubbed into the chest. I have seen Tiger balm on sale in Malaysia, Singapore, Thailand and Nepal, and you may well find it in a Chinese herbal or health-food shop. Use the general healing symbol (*see page 17*), then hold your hand on your chest and feel the warmth.

### Colds and flu

Have you been overdoing it? Colds and flu are a good way for your body to get a break without succumbing to a serious illness. Treat it as a sign and take time out. Colds can also be an indication of unshed tears. Are you bottling things up? If so, let your tears flow and see the cold as a way of letting go of that which your body no longer needs.

### Constipation

Do you go with the flow of life or do you like to control? Maybe you are holding on to your emotions and don't express your true feelings. You need to surrender to life and let go the reins.

I have been a control freak all my life. I love schedules and to-do lists and getting myself and others organised. I have had to work hard on this aspect of myself but it seems to be working! I also find that a bowl of unsweetened muesli every morning works wonders. You may find linseed helpful. The sweeping exercise (*see pages 73–4*) is a good one to try here, and use the healing symbol to bring in the energy to your sluggish bowels.

### Diabetes

Do you believe you are not getting enough love? Has life lost its sweetness? Work on self-love and appreciate all the little kindnesses that people do as signs of their love, even if they don't say the words of love to you directly.

### Eczema

As with psoriasis, this skin problem demonstrates a sensitivity between ourselves and the outside world. Sufferers are often shy and find it difficult to mix. If you are fearful of what others may think of you, spend some time prac- tising the exercises on self-worth and self-esteem (*see pages 27–8*). See yourself as a unique and special person and equal to all around you. Each one of us has some- thing different and special to bring to the world – don't underestimate your worth.

### Eyesight problems

If you have problems with your eyesight you may be suffering from a blinkered attitude. Are you shunning the outside world? Maybe you are fearful of what you will see if you look properly. The world can be a cruel and hard place and sometimes it is helpful to have a reason for not seeing it too clearly. Are you a realist or a dreamer? Do you see things clearly or are your attitudes and ideals blurred? Consider whether you have any fears that you haven't accepted about the world and your role in it.

### Gallstones

Are you bitter about something? Is there some deep resentment down there lurking in the depths? Did one of your parents leave when you were young? Forgive and let go the past.

### Headaches

These are often caused by pressure, whether at work or in your personal life. Do you feel overwhelmed? Are you worrying too much or overloading your life? You are very likely to be pressurising yourself somehow.

Check your neck because most stress is held in the neck and shoulders and this can pull vertebrae out of place and also cause headaches. Meditate: clear the aura of thought forms by using the sweeping exercise (*see pages 73–4*).

Watch your diet for too much coffee, chocolate and alcohol. Use the pendulum or kiniesiology muscle response exercise (*see pages 46–7 and 45–6*) to check which, if any, foods are upsetting you. Finally, drink lots of water as dehydration is a common cause of headaches.

### Heart problems

Do you respect and love yourself? Work on your self-esteem. Alternatively, you may be heart-sore – maybe you have had your heart broken by the loss of someone close. Heart problems are often associated with overwork so look at your lifestyle and working conditions. Are you stressed? Could you take it a little easier? Do you get enough gentle exercise? If you have had heart problems, I am sure you have been given plenty of medical guidance on how to cope. However, I would suggest you do the chakra balancing meditation daily (*see page 26*) and spend plenty of time on the heart centre part of the exercise.

### Indigestion and stomach ulcers

Do you bottle up your emotions? Are you worried about your performance? We tend to hold down our feelings and the difficult experiences of our past in our solar plexus region. We let things that annoy and irritate us fester away. This is where hate will sit and eat away at us. If we have taken something into our lives that doesn't really agree with us it can cause indigestion.

Try to live in the present and worry less about the future. I personally find that peppermint tea, either the readymade version or made fresh from boiling mint leaves, helps soothe the stomach. Use the digestive tract healing symbol (*see page 92*).

## Symbol for Digestive Tract Healing

This symbol encompasses the entire digestive tract so it can be used for any digestive disorder (hiatus hernia, candida, irritable bowel syndrome, etc.). It also helps to bring the tract into balance if it is too alkaline or too acid.

*Trace the symbol in the air in front of your trunk using both hands, moving up the body as many times as necessary.*

### Knee problems

Are you worried about some future plans? Are you nervous about taking the next step in your life? Check that the decisions you are making are really what you want – what you feel not what you think you want. Are you bottling up your emotions? Your knees (and your hips) can become stiff as a result of suppressed feelings. Use the exercise to release emotions (*see page 112*).

### Leg and feet problems

Are you feeling insecure? Do you feel supported? Are you worrying about your home or job? Our legs and feet need to be in full working order to take us forward in life, so if we are frightened of the future they can 'seize up'. During one of the busiest and most chaotic periods of my life I fell and damaged my knee. I was forced to lay up for a week – my body, mind and spirit got the rest it needed!

### Liver problems

Are you angry or easily upset? Do you have a quick temper? Are you irritable? Are you a nervous and anxious person? The liver is associated with anger – as in 'liverish'! Do you feel life has dealt you a poor hand? Use the exercise to release emotions (*see page 112*) and let your anger go. Any bitter herbal remedies are good for stimulation of the liver – try dandelion tea. Walnuts and grapefruit can also help.

### Myalgic encephalomyelitis (ME)

This condition is set off by a virus and it leaves the sufferer virtually unable to live a normal life. It brings extreme fatigue and a lack of purpose, apparently taking away all the aims and ambitions of the victim. The ME sufferer shows a complete detachment from the world.

ME can be caused by an overload of work or any other form of stress. It is a way of the body saying that it has had enough of the problems and challenges that a person's emotional, mental and spiritual bodies are undergoing. It is a great retreat because it is impossible to continue normal activity but in itself it is not life threatening.

If you suffer from this condition, you need to conduct a full review of your life and uncover the main cause of your stress. Take time out and follow all the exercises in this book as a complete healing is needed. Take small steps back into your life. Be kind to yourself.

## Neck stiffness

Are you slow to take on new ideas? Are you a bit stuck in your thinking or set in your ways? If so, do something totally spontaneous that, as a friend of mine always puts it, will 'make your heart sing'. Check that the problem is not due to your shoulders being out of kilter because they are taking on too many burdens. Massage will help you relax and unlock stiff muscles. Take time out and have some fun.

## Osteoporosis

This is a problem that is often faced by women after menopause. Brittle and porous bones – a weakening of the skeleton on which our body hangs – may be associated with a weakening of the support system in our life, like dropping down to a pensioner's income or the loss of a supporting partner. The ultimate result of osteoporosis is 'widow's hump', a distortion of the top of the spine.

Have you been carrying the problems and cares of family and friends for too long? Maybe you are unable to stand up and carry life's burdens any longer.

An impact activity will help prevent this problem – try aerobics, running, jogging or power walking. Interestingly, vegetarians rarely suffer from osteoporosis, as one of the causes is too much animal protein. Take a supplement of two parts calcium, one part magnesium. Soya products are also excellent for easing this condition.

## Panic attacks and emotional outbursts

Do you have needless fears? Do you worry about the future? Practise living in the moment. Enjoy what you are doing now and let the future evolve in its own time and in its own way, while realising that what will occur will be the best for you.

If you are a woman, check that your hormones are not out of balance due to the menopause or premenstrual tension, and consider taking supplements of vitamin B complex, vitamin B6 and natural HRT substitutes (available from your health-food shop or a naturopath). Regular meditation is another great help.

When the attacks come on, breathe deeply and use the sweeping exercise (*see pages 73–4*) to calm yourself down. The harmony symbol may help if there is chaos around you. Use this on yourself or draw it in your home and workplace to create a harmonious space around you.

I have found that the Bach Flower Rescue Remedy and Star of Bethlehem Remedy are also good for relieving panic and anxiety.

### Symbol for Harmony

This symbol will bring peace and harmony to a situation, person or home. Use it on yourself and where you live and work to create a harmonious space around you. It will clear chaos and the after-effects of arguments and aggression. It acts like a candle bringing peaceful light.

*Start drawing from the bottom, creating the base first, then move up the stem and draw the flame last of all.*

## Psoriasis

Are you over-sensitive to the problems of others, or do you worry too much about what people think of you? Use the egg exercise (*see pages 29–30*) to strengthen the outer wall of your auric field. Psoriasis often goes hand in hand with dryness of the skin so drink plenty of water and up your intake of essential fatty acids like flaxseed oil or fish oils.

## Rheumatism

Do you prevaricate? Do you put your plans and dreams into action or are you frightened of the consequences of making a move? When energy is stuck in the muscles and won't flow, it's a sign that you cannot take action without causing yourself pain. Write down all the things in life that you would love to do and then plan to put one thing on that short list into action. Be brave!

## Shoulder pain

Are you taking on too many responsibilities? Have you been taking the problems of others on to your shoulders? Visualise all these responsibilities and cares as stones, then see them falling off and feel yourself getting lighter.

## Sleep problems

If you suffer from insomnia or disturbed sleep, you probably have unresolved issues going around your head repeatedly. You may be consumed with anxiety and worries, and these get worse at night.

In chapter seven I have set out an exercise that will help you connect to your senses and take your mind off your concerns (*see pages 205–6*). Drink camomile tea before bedtime and avoid chocolate, tea, coffee or caffeinated fizzy drinks, as these are all stimulants. I would also avoid cheese as this can cause nightmares and disturbed sleep. Try using the peace and sleep symbol (see below) as I have found it most effective.

### Symbol for Peace or Sleep

This symbol was originally given to me to help someone with insomnia but it is also the peace symbol. Use it on yourself. If you find it difficult to draw while lying down, I suggest you visualise it running down your body.

*Visualise or draw the symbol in the air in front of you, working all the way down from your head to your feet. Do this as many times as you like.*

### Urinary infections and prostate problems

Are you holding on and not going with the flow of life? Are you uptight? Are you still living your life as you did when you were twenty years younger? Then update your thinking – remember that the ways of the past are not necessarily better than the ways of the present. Pumpkin seeds are a great snack and will help with all urinary problems. Saw palmetto is a good herbal remedy, especially for prostate problems, and cranberry juice will also help.

---

What we are today is a direct result of our past experiences, our attitudes to those experiences, our genetic inheritance, and the collective thoughts of ourselves and others.

---

The woman who told me this story is a rebirther from Holland. I met her in Malaysia when she was visiting Kuala Lumpur to give some healing sessions and workshops on the art of rebirthing – the technique of taking a person back to the time before their birth, to their mother's womb. A rebirther leads people through their birth experience and helps them handle any trauma that may have occurred during their birth and the early stages of their life. These events are usually pushed far back into our memory but they can have a powerful and often detrimental effect on our lives. The theory is that by taking us back and showing us what happened we can then release the effects of these early traumas.

The rebirther and I spent some time discussing the effect of a mother's thoughts and emotions on the foetus in the womb. She agreed that they could have a powerful effect. She then told me that she had been born with a crippled left leg and had worn a leg iron as a child. In her youth she had determined to overcome this defect and, through exercise and self-healing techniques, she had more or less restored her leg to full health.

The woman married and had seven children, all of

rather than one which would look good on my CV. It was a good move – I met a wonderful group of people and started to enjoy my work again. I decided that I didn't need a man to make me happy and started a mini 'club' of women who were without partners. We would meet each week at a different restaurant and some of us would go on to a club and dance the night away.

As these things tend to happen, as soon as I let go the need for a man in my life, my future husband came into my life. Needless to say, my physical problems left me as well. I had let go the past and moved on into new experiences. I had let go my fear.

## Making use of your experiences

I often refer to our past experiences as our assets of today. We learn and grow from our experiences whether they inspired us at the time or challenged us. I would like to share with you an exercise that I did in preparation for my Wise Woman initiation ceremony in the Native American tradition, a beautiful rite of passage that was performed for me by my friend Daniel Derby, who is part Native American.

It's a ceremony that honours the older woman and demonstrates her value to herself and others. It is just what most of us need after we leave child rearing and step into the age of grandmother, as we can often feel that we have little left to offer. As a rite of passage, it takes us into the phase of our life where we can be a natural counsellor and share our wisdom with the younger members of our family and society in general.

In the ceremony I shared my past and the wisdom that it had given me. It was a beautiful experience. I wrote a poem about the life of a woman, which I read to the group of women friends who had come to share the occasion with me. They then gave me symbolic gifts of power and wisdom by handing me words – like 'tolerance', 'patience' and 'compassion' – on beautifully crafted cards. In order to acknowledge the wisdom I had accrued through my life, I had to write down all the major events in my life, the lessons I had learned from them and the skills I had acquired.

It was a heartening and uplifting exercise as it gave credence to all that had sometimes seemed negative in my past. I also found it interesting to note that many seemingly small and unimportant experiences had, in fact, had a profound effect upon me.

I invite you now to review your own life and discover the gifts that your experiences have given you.

---

EXERCISE: REVIEW YOUR LIFE'S EXPERIENCES

You will need to give yourself at least an hour for this exercise. I promise you it will be well worth your time.

- Take pen and paper and find yourself a quiet place.
- Go back in time to the very beginning of your life and write down every memorable event, whether happy or otherwise.
- Remember what happened and then write down what that experience gave you – what lesson you learned, what strength you gained.
- Share what you have written with your family and close ones, if you wish. It may give them insights into you and your past that will create stronger bonds between you. You might want to encourage them to do this exercise for themselves.

---

Very often it is the way that we handle the experiences of life that renders them either positive or negative events for ourselves and for those close to us. If we handle our emotions successfully, we create less harm for all involved. However, some feelings are difficult to control, and I would like to consider some of these now. We shall also look at ways in which we can release the emotional charge attached to memories of our past.

## Anger

Let's begin with the most destructive of all emotions – anger, and its bigger brother, hate. There are two aspects of anger that I would like us to consider. First, we'll look at the reasons why we get angry and, second, how we handle it when it rises up within us.

Spiritual teachers of the past and present tell us that we should be aiming for a point where we feel no anger. Unfortunately, most of us are nowhere near that point! In all the classes I have given, I have only ever come across a couple of people who say they have no anger and feel no anger.

Some of us flare up more quickly than others, and some people are slow boilers – they simmer for a while then burst out. I was always the quick and fiery type. As soon as something upset me I would burst out and then minutes later it would all be over.

What type are you? Do you simmer and moither over things or do you flare up instantly? Do you hold on to your anger for some time after the argument or event that caused your outburst? However you manifest your anger, I am sure you will agree that it isn't a good feeling and that afterwards you feel down and weakened by the outburst. You may even feel ashamed of yourself for losing control. We often say things that we later regret when we are in the centre of our anger. I never write or make phone calls when I am in that state for exactly that reason – I wait to see how I feel a little later, then I make my protest.

---

It's not wrong to give vent to your anger. You should never repress it – the repression is what makes you sick and is what turns anger into hate. Just try to minimise the effect: beat the pillow not the man.

---

Why do we get angry? One of the main reasons – and you may not like to hear this – is that we are actually cross with ourselves. Whoa – that's a hard pill to swallow. But let's take a look at a typical anger-inducing scenario.

You are late for an appointment and get stuck in a traffic jam. The man behind you starts to toot you, then the children start to quarrel. Whether you lose your temper at the traffic in front, the man behind or the children – you get mad. Why? There are often traffic jams and you don't lose your cool every time you get into one (or you'd be totally neurotic by now). The man behind is tooting but probably not at you so why should you care? – it's his problem. Why blame the children? – they obviously have their own problems if they are quarrelling and it's not directed at you. So why get so mad? Why go over the top? Could it be that you are mad with yourself for being late?

If you had allowed plenty of time, the traffic jam would not be a problem, the silly man behind would merely be an exasperated motorist, and the children would just be mildly irritating because of the noise they are making. It is within ourselves that the anger starts.

## Self-induced stress that causes anger

Much of our stress comes from not allowing enough time for the events on our daily planner. We create this stress as we take on too much in too little time. How much is really necessary and how often is it imperative that things get done at the time and speed that we dictate? Ease up on yourself and be philosophical about your daily schedule.

One day I realised I had forty-two things on my to-do list. I decided to tear it up. Now I have a couple of yellow stickers that remind me of the really important things I have to do. I have less stress now, yet I do more than I have ever done. I just don't worry about it. I occasionally make a mistake and miss an appointment but it's rare. I now add twenty-five per cent on to the time I think any journey or event will take, and life has become much easier.

---

**Every dispute is a matter of perspective.**

---

## Other causes of anger

What are the other causes of anger? Under analysis, I can guarantee that ninety per cent of the time your anger will be with yourself and not with another person. People don't usually try to induce anger. In fact, the opposite is true – it's bad for business.

Sometimes people's lack of concern or lack of attention

to detail may be upsetting, but this is because you are looking at things from your perspective and with your standards not theirs. If you don't like the way a company operates then either don't use them again or write or ring and complain – but not when you are angry. Do it when you have cooled down.

Sit down now and make a list of all the things that either have made you angry in the last month or make you angry in principle. Check them all carefully. Do you have a really good reason for those heightened emotions?

---

**The people around us are our mirrors.**

---

Think about this every time you get angry. Do you get angry with your partner when you are running late? Should you have allowed more time, especially as you know your partner always takes an hour to get ready? Do you get angry in the car when you are lost? Should you have bought a map, or called for directions? Do you get angry when there isn't enough money in the bank? Do you feel guilty about your lack of contribution or your spending?

There are, of course, situations that are not your fault, even if we take the point that we send out vibrations of energy that attract our situations. When dealing with national and global events, we are faced with mankind's collective thought forms and if these don't harmonise with our own thoughts and feelings we are likely to get upset. That's good. We can get angry about the cruel treatment of elephants in Malaysia, about bears being farmed for bile in China, about governments wasting money on armaments, about child abuse, and so on.

I was very angry when the terrorists flew into the World Trade Center in New York, and also when I saw the plight of the Afghani refugees. I honestly feel that the anger we feel about these types of situation is good. It exists to spur us into action. Anger and fear in the primal state are produced for fight-and-flight action and exist for our survival. So use that anger and turn it into action. Write letters of protest, vote with your feelings, and send money to support the causes that trouble you. Do something. Action will help relieve the frustration and anger you feel.

This is a story about an old friend of mine who is as about as placid as a person can be. She is tolerant, understanding and a great big bundle of love. In the thirty years that I have known her, I have never even known her to raise her voice. However, there is another side to her nature! My friend once told me about a time when she was younger and, while walking in her neighbourhood after school, came across a group of teenage boys taunting and teasing a younger child. As she approached them, her emotions built up and suddenly she found she couldn't see properly – her vision was impaired by a film of red, as if she were looking through glasses with red lenses. She felt two metres tall and as if she had the strength of Tarzan. She stalked straight up to the teenagers, who were a threatening bunch, and set about them with her satchel, screaming at the top of her voice for them to stop. She said she could have torn them apart if she had to, she felt so strong.

The boys fled – from my demure and gentle friend, who was twelve years old at the time! In this case, anger gave my friend the energy and strength of spirit to act. Well done, Lyn!

On a day-to-day basis, whether the anger you feel is against yourself or against another, it is better out than in. I don't advocate physical or verbal abuse against the perpetrator. Don't go and knock his teeth in! This won't help a thing – the energies will just be sent back to you. But let it go in a harmless way. Try thumping a pillow.

> Suppressed anger is pure corrosive.

## Recognising your anger

On your list of reasons why you get angry you may have included one or two of the following:

- **Embarrassment** When you do something that doesn't fit with your normal code of behaviour and you care about what other people are saying or thinking about you.
- **Frustration** When events are not going the way you planned so you feel out of control.
- **Irritation** When other people's habits and actions don't match with your terms of good behaviour.
- **Shock** When someone says something about you that isn't true.
- **Concern** When you see someone you care for being mistreated.

This list suggests two types of situation: one where we see things from a different perspective than other people, and another where we are being kick-started into some action to redress a problem. When you are angry, recognise this.

Realise that your anger is being caused by your attitude – I am not saying this attitude is wrong, but it is your own – or take action. But remember not to do anything when you are in the heat of the anger – it will be harmful to you and harmful to others, and you will always regret it later. Cool down first.

## Letting go of old anger

Old anger is more difficult to let go of, but the exercise I am about to show you has proved to be most effective and can be life changing. It involves you committing your emotions to paper, which you then burn. I have done this exercise with many people and they have all felt great benefit. It gives you a chance to say and express those feelings that you cannot necessarily express directly to the person involved.

When we burn the writing I always feel the release of the energy attached to the issues that are burning – it is astonishing how each person's will burn differently. You may find you need to do the exercise many times to let go of all your past pain, hurt, trauma, anger, bitterness and even hate. Don't worry if you cry while you are doing this. Tears are the greatest form of release. You can also use this exercise to get rid of current anger.

Here is the release symbol, which will help you release your old emotions and pain. You will be using it in the following exercise while you watch your writing go up in flames.

### Symbol for Releasing
This symbol will assist in the releasing of suppressed emotions, old wounds and angry thought forms. It is also

useful for any form of congestion – from a stuffy nose
to constipation – and can help to relax tense muscles and
soothe cramps.

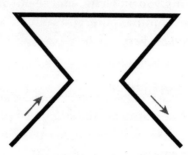

*Trace the release symbol from the left to the right in the air
in front of you. Do this three times.*

---

EXERCISE: RELEASE YOUR OLD EMOTIONS
You will need some kind of incinerator for this exercise.
It can be any heatproof container, like an old saucepan
or a large flowerpot.

* Take pen and paper and find yourself a quiet place
  where you won't be disturbed.
* Write down all the feelings you have about events in
  your past that have hurt or disturbed you. If you
  wish, you can write this in the form of a letter to the
  person who has hurt you.
* Write down everything; don't hold back. This is your
  chance to let rip.
* When you are sure you have finished, roll the paper
  up and, preferably outside, set light to the end of it
  and drop it into your heatproof container.
* As the paper burns and the smoke rises, know that
  you are letting go of the emotions written on that
  paper. Draw the release symbol over the flames to help

## Rational and irrational fear

There are two types of fear: rational and irrational. We are born with the rational, natural fear of heights and loud noises. These fears are survival fears. If we get too close to a high ledge we may fall over, and loud noises alert us to the possibility of danger.

Of course, it is good to be cautious and careful with our great gift of life. However, if we get over-cautious or over-fearful then our life becomes stunted and we cannot move forward or grow. We become frightened of stepping into life's experiences, which we need in order to grow and develop our character and soul. If you were knocked down by a car as a child, for example, then you might be naturally more wary of crossing a road than the next person. But if you have become paranoid and too frightened to cross the road, your fear has taken control of you.

There are two things to note here. Firstly, the events of our past took place when we were in a different state from the one we are in now – because we are changing all the time. So there is no reason why any event should reoccur. The second is that if you keep thinking of something over and over you will end up creating the situation you fear. That is how life works; what we think we create.

## What do you fear?

I believe that behind most of our issues – our problems in life – we will find a fear lurking. In other words, we may be angry with someone, or feel helpless, or inadequate but if we look a little deeper we will probably find that our surface emotion is hiding a deeper one – fear.

Take the example of the young hooligans who are terrorising our inner cities and causing havoc after football matches. These youngsters tend to move around in large groups and have a macho image. They seem angry and they are obviously destructive, but I would suggest that it is fear that motivates their behaviour – fear of being alone, fear of rejection by their peers, fear of inadequacy.

We all mask our deepest fears with outward bravado and put on acts from time to time. But if we are to heal truly we need to look deep within ourselves and be honest about our feelings. I instinctively look beneath the surface of anyone I meet when I see anger or a hurtful attitude, to see what the person is fearing. Here are some thoughts for you to ponder on . . .

In your home life:
- Do you resent your parents or your siblings?
- Were you or are you fearful of not getting enough love and attention from your parents?
- Do you think that deep down you don't deserve your parents' love?
- Do you have deep-seated fears that reflect low self-esteem?

In your working environment:
- Do you get impatient with your colleagues or with processes, whether they are the banking system, legal system or local government?
- Why do you get cross with other people's inadequacies and lack of professionalism? Is what you see in them something you fear in yourself?
- Are you fearful of failure at work? Check to see if you are in the right job.

- Do you rush around the office and take on more than you can cope with? Is this perhaps a sign of lack of confidence? Are you in the right position? Are you afraid to say that you can't cope with your workload?

In everyday situations:
- When you get impatient with traffic queues, what is it that you actually fear? Could it be that you fear that someone will think you are rude for being late? Are you fearful that you have not met your high standards of timekeeping – are you a perfectionist?
- Will you not love or respect yourself if you don't live up to these standards? Are these standards props in your life that you have put up to keep the fear of inadequacy out?

In your relationships:
- Do you fear that your partner will leave you?
- Do you have confidence that you can support yourself?
- Do you fear that your partner will be more successful than you?
- Do you fear that your partner will lose respect for you if you do not 'succeed' at your work?
- Do you fear that your partner will grow tired of you or no longer find you attractive?
- Do you fear that if you love too much then you may lose the object of your love?

Only when we are honest with ourselves about our deeper feelings can we tackle the fears that lurk beneath the surface. Over the next few weeks I suggest you watch yourself carefully – as soon as your temperature starts to rise, note what set if off. Then when you have a quiet moment, analyse your reactions and see if you can work out what your underlying fears are.

You need to overcome as many of these 'attitudes' as possible – even getting mad in a traffic jam – because they give you stress. They bring you off balance. They take you off track. Peace does not come from getting wound up by a late train or a lazy civil servant or a greedy lawyer. If you know what it is you fear, you can start to come to terms with it. Once you have overcome the fear, you will find you can overcome your reactions to the 'button pushing' events in your life.

A young girl was once brought to me by her anxious and concerned brothers. She was incredibly thin and they couldn't understand why. I asked the girl if she ate properly and she told me that she did. I scanned her with my hands and looked for any emotional block that might have been troubling her. It took me a while but I eventually picked up fear. I asked her again if she was eating properly. This time she said no and said it was because she couldn't – she just couldn't get the food down. I started to ask a little more about her life.

The girl was a bright student and her family had great expectations of her becoming an accountant. I asked her gently whether she was afraid of failing her exams and letting her family down. Her eyes filled with tears and she acknowledged that this was her great fear. Her family was poor and if she succeeded she would bring them honour and advantages – the responsibility she felt was great. I quietly told her that she could let her fear go and I felt a huge energy shift as it left her.

Just talking to someone about her fears and having the space to acknowledge the weight of her responsibilities was enough to release the girl's pent-up feelings. I told her brothers about her worries and they both assured her of their support. She promised them that she would start to eat again – of course, she now felt she could as she had let go all that fear and darkness within her.

## Unreasonable fears

I mentioned earlier that our soul is on a cycle – a journey through life on Earth, then through death, into the spirit world then back through rebirth again. This means that we have had many, many lives before this current one. We normally don't remember the events of our past but memories of past events from these lives are hidden deep in our subconscious. One of the results of this is that we may be affected by fears that can seem totally irrational but are actually founded in the past.

I am a great believer in facing fear and defying it. I find this not only overcomes my fear but also makes me strong. Most of my fears came with me at my birth. Once I started healing I realised that most people cannot point to a reason for many of their fears or phobias. When I am healing someone I often see their past lives flashing in front of me, rather like video clips in my mind. This was what made me realise that a lot of our fears originate in our previous lives. They may have been caused by events of the past that are long forgotten by our conscious mind, but our soul and higher self remembers them and the cause of them. When faced with a similar cause, we have a naturally fearful reaction.

Here are some of the fears people have described to me:

Fear of:
- Flying
- Water
- Small, enclosed spaces
- Healing
- Public speaking
- Crowds
- Men
- Being smothered
- Fire
- Having children

Do you suffer from any of these? Take a moment and think about your irrational fears. Write them down – let's see if we can work through them and let them go.

## Fear is the barrier to our progress in life

I used to fear horses, tunnels and caves, spiral staircases, public speaking, priests and church personnel. I then had a session with a therapist who, through a form of hypnosis, took me back to a past life and allowed me to see in my imagination – my inner eye – events from that life.

The experience was a little like watching a video of events taking place around me in the past. I had one life where I ran out of a house in London, somewhere similar to Piccadilly. I ran straight out in front of a carriage drawn by six or eight black horses. The last thing I remember seeing were the horses' hooves coming down to crush me.

Once I realised that my horse experience was so far in the past it seemed ridiculous for me to be bothered by it now. However, the fact was that I was still terrified of horses and my heart would start to pound whenever I came close to them.

My first attempt to overcome the fear of horses didn't come to much but it got me on the right road: I went horse riding with some friends in South Africa. I was given a very, very docile horse to ride. It was so docile I spent the whole hour sitting on its back 20 metres from the stables, waiting for it to move. Of course, the horse thought he was having a great day and had a little nap! But it was a start.

The main breakthrough came when I was in Egypt on holiday with a friend. We rushed to see the pyramids on our first day and were faced with a choice: we could go across the desert to see them on either a camel or a horse. I took one look at the camel and decided on the horse. It all happened so quickly I didn't have time to think and before I knew it, there I was trotting around the pyramids – so completely overawed by them that I forgot my fear. And now I live in the middle of the New Forest in England where ponies run wild and walk down our lane all day and night.

My holiday in Egypt also gave me the opportunity to face another of my fears. We were offered the chance to spend the night in the Great Pyramid of Cheops. I knew it would be a wonderful experience, but I couldn't think how I would get through the tunnels. I couldn't do a full past-life regression because I would have needed a trained therapist.

I spoke to one of our colleagues on the trip, Ken Page, who is a well-known and accomplished healer in the United States. Ken suggested I try a quick and simple way of discovering what caused my fear. I followed his instructions and, lo and behold, I saw myself as a small boy in a mine and the roof fell down and smothered me. I could now understand my fear and I used his technique to send the fear away. It worked well for me and I spent one of the most illuminating nights of my life in the pyramid – but that's another story.

Here's the technique that Ken showed me – if you have no success in finding the source of the fear then just do the second part, which is to let go and release it.

---

EXERCISE: RELEASE YOUR FEAR
- Find yourself a quiet place, sit down and close your eyes.
- Think of the fear that you wish to let go.
- Throw your eyes up to the sky (still with your eyes closed). What do you see? Don't stop to think about it – see the first thing that comes into your head.
- Hold the image in your imagination for a few moments. If you don't see anything in particular, just concentrate on the fear.
- Imagine that the scene or fear is engulfed by a large ball of light. The light creates a balloon in which the fear floats.
- Release the ball of light as you would a helium balloon. See it float to the Sun. Use the release symbol (*see page 112*) to assist you, drawing it three times.
- When the balloon hits the Sun, see it burst and feel your fear disperse for ever.
- Watch as golden rain pours down from the balloon and covers you – the rain is the wisdom and the understanding that you have gained from experiencing the fear.
- Repeat the exercise as many times as necessary.

---

I overcame my fears by using this mind exercise, and also by physically forcing myself to face what was frightening me. If you can bring yourself to do this you will find tremendous relief — it really is very empowering to get on top of a fear. It's an indicator that you are in control of your life and that you are your own master. For further help with overcoming fear read Susan Jeffers's excellent book *Feel the Fear and Do it Anyway*.

Now you have worked through the blocks and the source of your problems, you are ready to start learning to love yourself at every level — to care for and cherish yourself on a day-to-day basis. Let's continue our healing journey by taking a closer look at love and what it can do for us.

# 4

# Loving and Respecting Yourself

Our self-esteem is the foundation on which we can begin our healing. In this chapter we look at ways to love and respect ourselves. Only when we have learned to give ourselves the love we deserve can we can move forward into balanced and sharing relationships with other people. We consider the different kinds of love in our lives and look at ways to love unconditionally.

Before we can truly heal ourselves we have to establish our self-esteem, self-appreciation and self-love. If we can learn to love ourselves, we can evolve spiritually and become our true selves. Once we have repaired the damage of the past to our self-esteem, we can open ourselves to the love of others.

The more you love and respect yourself the more you can love and respect others.

## *Self-esteem*

One of the major causes of unhappiness and lack of motivation is low self-esteem. From the moment we are born we are inspected, judged and valued. Our skills are examined and our bodies are placed under scrutiny. We are told we are good, bad, too fat, too thin, lazy, beautiful, clever, stupid. We cannot help but start to judge ourselves. We open magazines and we see pictures of how society (through the eyes of the media) would like to see us – what the perfect person wears, the ideal dimensions, what our hair colour should be and how long we should grow our nails.

It's not surprising that we find ourselves less than perfect when compared with these airbrushed images of perfection. We go to work and we are expected to achieve; we are shown pie charts and graphs that plot our success and failure. We turn on the television and we see young people like ourselves in fast cars and big homes, happy and smiling with perfect partners, and perfect children with cornflakes dribbling down their chins. No wonder we get down on ourselves when we are constantly faced with the ideal package.

### Images we strive to recreate

The fact is that we live in an era in which we are continually barraged with visions of the perfect lifestyle and the perfect body, not to mention the comments of our peers, who see these visions too and expect us to live up to them. Sadly, the less people live up to these perceived standards themselves the more likely they are to find fault with others. It's human nature: the fat man will laugh at the fatter man because it makes him feel better about himself.

What kind of society is it that presents an eighteen-year-old soap star as a perfect female role model, or a youth who can kick a ball around a field as the ideal male? What happened to the true values of life? What happened to judging someone by how much love they give, how much they help others, their beautiful smile, how gentle they are, etc.?

The truth is that these values still exist but they are being corroded by the superficial messages pumped out by our mass media. The papers may give out 'Best Grannie' awards, but they still proclaim 36, 24, 36 as the perfect female figure and push it in our faces. Loving attitudes and caring people are still in demand and still valued – it's just unfortunate that the media pays so much attention to looks and image these days.

You may wonder why I am getting so heated. It's because I see the results: the children who have been brainwashed into thinking they are of no value. I see hundreds of men and women who have little or no self-esteem and who as a result are anything from anxious to suicidal.

Are you one of these people? Do you punish yourself with unnatural diets and exercise routines because you are determined to be the perfect size 10? Do you work around the clock so that you can be the best at what you do? Do you do a job you hate because you believe no one else will employ you? Do you hate your hair, your figure, your feet? Do you think less of yourself because you find public speaking difficult? Do you hate yourself because you can't do maths, or can't sing, or can't run fast, or hate large crowds, or, or, or . . . ?

Do you find it difficult:
• To love yourself?
• To respect yourself?
• To value yourself?

If you have answered yes to any of these three questions, you are suffering (in common with the majority of the population) from less than perfect self-esteem. You may even have *low* self-esteem. If you suffer from depression then this is extremely likely.

## Feeling Good about Yourself

I would like to say now that, whatever you think of yourself, *I know you are OK*. I know you are doing it right; I know you are a beautiful soul, because you cannot be anything else. There is no wrong way to look, to dress, to act or to be. It's all right. Your way or look may be different from other people's but it is you so it's OK.

---

Concern yourself with your own perception of who you are and not with how others see you – their perception is based only on an external view of you.

---

If I were to ask you now to write down the ten things you most dislike about yourself, you would probably snatch up some paper and start scribbling away instantly. Sorry, I'm not going to ask you do that – it would be far too easy!

---

EXERCISE: RAISE YOUR SELF-ESTEEM
- Find a quiet place and sit down with paper and pen.
- Write down everything you can possibly think of that's good about you and that you can do well. Are you good with children, for example? Do you have

green fingers, cook a mean pasta, smile easily, etc.?

- When you have completed that list, start a new one, this time writing down all the things you have ever done for other people (including your family and friends). Have you ever remembered a friend's birthday, for example? Do you ever give to charity? Have you ever cooked someone a meal or given them a bed for the night? Have you stopped to help someone who is lost or whose car has broken down? I'm sure you will recall many little things – and some big ones as well – that you have done for other people.

- When you've finished, give yourself credit for being a beautiful soul and hug yourself. Keep the lists somewhere you can find them easily whenever you start to feel less of yourself.

---

You can also do this exercise with a close friend. Make a list of each other's good points then swap the lists. You'll be surprised how many good things your friend sees in you.

On a day-to-day basis, start to see the good in yourself and treat yourself as you would someone you love. Don't judge yourself against others but remember that you are unique. Spoil yourself occasionally. Give yourself space to do the things you enjoy, and allow yourself a little time just for you every day. If you are a woman, have the odd beauty treatment, pamper yourself from time to time. As you start to treat yourself better you will notice that other people will as well, especially your family. I am asking you to be a little more self-centred – not selfish, but self-centred. By changing yourself you will change the way life treats you.

## Look at your lifestyle

By this point in our journey of self-awareness you will have realised that I am a great believer in self-responsibility: I believe that we create our own happiness and we create the life we need and want. With positive thinking and by relying on feelings rather than logic, we create the world we desire. I am now going to ask you to take a look at the way you treat yourself on a physical level. I want you to consider the way your chosen lifestyle is affecting your health and your emotional stability.

I recently read in *Conversations with God* by Neale Donald Walsch that if we smoke, drink alcohol or take drugs 'we don't wish to live'. It seemed a harsh statement at first, but after consideration I realised its core of truth. If we truly cherish our life then we will do everything we possibly can to enhance and prolong it. We all know that excessive smoking, drinking and drug taking is detrimental to our health. In the same way, over-eating and excess sugar and fat will put a strain on our physical system and can eventually cause premature death. However, in most privileged countries our everyday lives are full of temptations to over-indulge in one way or another.

I recognise that for the highest good of our physical bodies – and therefore in respect of our soul – we should refrain from smoking, drinking alcohol and taking drugs. However, I am of the moderate school of thinking. I believe that if we can keep all these things in moderation and avoid dependency then we can still be happy and contented, peaceful and loving. If you are planning to move speedily along your spiritual path, then you may consider a purer lifestyle. But since this book is written for people who are doing their best to get through to next year let alone reach the zenith of existence, I shall continue to recommend moderation rather than abstinence.

## Sleep, snoozes and catnaps

Although I know Mrs Thatcher managed to run Britain on four hours sleep a night, I personally need at least seven. As you get older you may find that you can't manage so many late nights and all-night raves, so don't fight it. Let your body take what it needs and sleep as much as you have to. Listen to your body: it will tell you when it's not getting enough of anything or if it's getting too much. If you need help with insomnia, I would suggest you look to herbal remedies (I don't believe in sleeping pills). You will find these in most health-food shops.

Apart from needing sleep, our bodies also require plenty of rest and relaxation. When I am travelling and have a full and arduous schedule, often beginning at seven in the morning and ending at eleven at night, I find catnaps a useful way to revitalise myself. Again, as I have said before, don't be put off by your upbringing and conditioning. So many people I know think it is a sin to go to bed in the daytime! If you feel tired and it's possible for you to get to a bed – make the most of it and have a snooze. Even in the office environment you can often close the door and have yourself a quick nap. I find it a wonderful way to regenerate myself.

---

Treat yourself as you would a dear old friend who needs love and attention, because that is exactly what you are.

---

## Take a break

If you feel you need a break then do nothing for the weekend: let the weeds grow, don't cut the grass, cancel the dinner party – just do nothing. My husband has been my greatest teacher when it comes to relaxation. He sees no reason to be always doing: he can sit still in a chair and daydream for hours. I have always been the great doer, the creator of to-do lists, the let's-find-a-project person who wants to see how much we can do in one day before we fall over with exhaustion. But now I can also do nothing – it's not easy but I can do it!

Take a look at the way animals live their lives. They don't have agendas, issues or timetables. They just are. They follow their instincts and live in the moment.

We spend a great deal of our time thinking about the past, mulling over the 'what ifs' and 'I should haves', and planning for the future – both are mind-sets that induce worry and stress. There is rarely stress in the vital moment of now, unless you are about to be sprung upon by a crouching lion, and such things don't happen that often in Surbiton. So take a break and relax.

---

Our imagination is the communication system between our higher self and our consciousness – listen to what it brings.

---

## Meditation as a way to relax

Meditation can help us relax and give us a chance to go deep within ourselves. I always feel better after I have closed my eyes, taken a few deep breaths and let my mind follow a theme or story. My imagination will take me away from my everyday concerns into another land – one that cannot be seen with the naked eye but which still exists for me. These realms are as real as you want them to be. Don't worry about the whys and wherefores, just enjoy the ride.

This next exercise will help you relax and also to love yourself a little more.

---

EXERCISE: CONNECT WITH YOUR INNER STRENGTH
This exercise is meant to help you relax so take your time about it. The pauses can be as long as you need them to be – providing you don't zone out completely and lose track of where you are in the meditation.

- Find a quiet place and close your eyes. Drop your shoulders and completely relax.
- Breathe in deeply four times. As you breathe in, imagine that you are breathing in white light and that it brings you peace and calm. As you breathe out, watch all your cares and worries leave you like puffs of smoke, creating clouds that rise up to the sky and are dissolved by the Sun.
- Pause for a few moments.
- See roots growing out of the bottom of your feet, as if you were a tree.
- Imagine that the roots are growing down into the ground beneath you.
- Pause.
- Know that you are totally connected to the Earth.
- Pause.
- Now imagine that you are walking through a wood on a sunny day.

- See the Sun dappling through the branches, creating pools of light on the path ahead. Hear the sound of water in the distance. As you carry on walking, the sound of the water gets louder.
- Eventually you step into a large clearing. You see a wonderful sight in front of you: the Sun shining on a beautiful waterfall that is tumbling over into a magical pool.
- Watch as the Sun catches the spray and it falls like diamonds all around you.
- Feel excited and childlike as you take off your clothes and leap into the pool.
- Feel the water cascade over you and feel all your inhibitions and cares wash away.
- Let the water clear away your self-doubts and lack of confidence. Decide which aspects of yourself you are going to let go. Stay in the water until you feel thoroughly cleansed.
- Feeling lighter and totally refreshed, look up and see the entrance to a cave in a rock behind the waterfall.
- Climb up to the cave entrance and step inside.
- Notice the clear crystal light that sparkles and throws rainbows across the cave.
- On the far side of the cave see a magnificent being – a person of stature and strength, who is filled with confidence and glowing with love and wellbeing.
- Watch as the person steps towards you with arms outstretched. As they move closer, realise that it is you – the powerful, balanced and capable aspect of you, filled with self-respect and love.
- Let this aspect of you walk right into you. Embrace this new you that is everything you would ever want to be, and let it completely merge with your being.

Know that you are a unique and very special person. Cherish yourself.

- Pause.
- Now slowly, and in your own time, leave the cave and the pool and make your way back into the room, bringing with you this new-found inner strength, harmony and self-respect.

---

Let's now look at ways we can continue to build on our self-esteem in our daily lives, and consider the ways we can nurture and love our bodies.

## A loving and healthy environment

I'm probably not the best person to be talking about mess as I'm not the tidiest person around, but it's definitely worth a mention. If we hoard, and surround ourselves with old books, papers and unused clothes, etc., we have to ask ourselves whether this is a reflection of what is going on in our lives generally. If you haven't used something for two years are you likely to use it again? If there is any doubt I suggest you get rid of it!

The clutter in your life prevents new and maybe more exciting things moving in. So have a good clear out. Cleaning out your cupboards is an excellent cleansing and releasing process that will affect you on all levels: emotional, mental, physical and spiritual.

In addition, check that you are keeping your sleeping space clear of electromagnetic equipment. The wave-bands that it emits can disturb the energy around you and this is particularly undesirable in the room where you sleep. Move the television out into the kitchen or living room, and avoid using a clock radio – a good old-fashioned wind-up alarm clock is by far the better option. The colours you choose to decorate your home can also affect your wellbeing. Every colour vibrates at a different wavelength of energy so opt for soft and relaxing ones when buying paint or wallpaper. Green and blue are healing colours so they make a great choice. Yellow will lift your spirits, whereas black will bring you down and red is a power colour so it could unsettle you. Don't let fashion dictate your surroundings but choose your colours according to how they make you feel.

## Love yourself with food

If we want to love ourselves it's important that we feed ourselves well and nurture our bodies. Let us treasure this 'temple of the soul', which is a wonderful description of the human frame. Boring though it may seem, we are to a great extent a product of what we eat.

We all know that we should minimise our intake of sugar and fat. I personally have felt much fitter since I became a vegetarian – one day the thought of eating something that had once been alive appalled me, and I haven't been able to take meat since then.

I would recommend that you try to eat organic food whenever possible, to avoid the toxicity in the food chain caused by the use of so many pesticides and chemical fertilisers. I also suggest you avoid highly processed foods if you can, since these do very little for your health. However, many books and numerous articles have been written about diet and nutrition and I don't intend to patronise you by telling you what you should or shouldn't eat here. I would like instead to give you a little advice, which is based on my healing experience of ailments caused by diet.

Many people seem to suffer from food sensitivities and allergies these days. The probable reason is that our food chain has become toxic through the extensive use of pesticides and weed killers, which have infiltrated the farmlands all over the planet. It is important for your comfort, let alone your health, to identify your sensitivities and give your body a rest from the particular foods that cause you problems.

I become totally exhausted when I eat too much bread, for example. The wheat and the yeast both give me problems and when my system gets overloaded I suffer from indigestion and constipation, which leads to toxicity and lack of energy. For a while I avoided bread completely, and now I can take it in small quantities. It is interesting to note that bread is also my main cause of weight gain.

I suspected for some time that I had intolerance to wheat, but it was a nutritionist who confirmed it for me, using a hair test. She took a small sample of my hair and sent it to a laboratory for testing. She also found I was intolerant to oats, barley and rye, and dairy products. These are not unusual sensitivities and I have met many people with the same problem. One of the side effects of dairy foods can be mucus, so if you suffer from sinusitis or catarrh then it may be a good idea to leave dairy products alone for a while and see if your condition improves.

I suggested in chapter two that you use muscle response testing to establish whether you are sensitive to any foods. If you don't feel that you can do this confidently for yourself then I advise you to visit a trained therapist. These days many nutritionists use this method of diagnosis. If you are having bouts of unexplained tiredness, anxiety, indigestion or just feelings of being under par then I recommend you visit one.

I have also found that the occasional fast or detoxification is a great way to raise my energy levels. This might not be the most pleasant medicine – pity I can't recommend a bar of chocolate a day for the same purpose! – but it gives good results.

The idea with a fast is to give your digestive system a break, a chance to recover from the onslaught it suffers day after day, especially when we overeat processed foods and take caffeinated drinks and alcohol. If you visit your nearest health-food shop you will find there are many detoxification products available. It is not a process you should undertake very often, but going without food for one day a month will keep your body clear.

Needless to say, I also recommend you limit your intake of coffee and tea, as although caffeine gives you an immediate lift, it is toxic in the long term. The same goes for chocolate, sweets and, of course, alcohol. Herbal teas and fruits are much better for you – sorry! If you can't refrain completely then indulge in moderation. And don't forget to drink plenty of water.

Try not to get obsessed with your diet and weight. If you find you are bingeing or denying yourself food when you need it, ask yourself why. Are you really concerned with your appearance and health or do you have an underlying problem that you are masking with your eating habits?

---

**Love your body and enjoy it – it's the best you'll get this time around. Feed it well and treat it with care.**

---

## Eating disorders

Eating disorders are a growing problem today, particularly in young women. Generally speaking, the medical profession relate such problems to childhood traumas and unfortunate comments made by parents, teachers or doctors. I believe that if a person has a balanced attitude to life and has well-developed self-esteem they will be able to take a few disparaging comments thrown their way in childhood. However, if someone has a nervous disposition or they have been abused in any serious way then bulimia and anorexia are more likely to develop.

If you know anyone who you suspect is suffering from either of these conditions, encourage them to let go their pent-up emotions and fears and give them as much love as you possibly can. As with all mental illness, telling someone to pull themselves together is not the answer. People need an inordinate amount of love and understanding. Don't be fobbed off by their excuses for why they are like they are – very often the underlying causes are deeply hidden and they need to be exposed with great care and a lot of help. Most mental illnesses and eating disorders point to a lack of self-love or respect.

## Letting go of our addictions

Just as a poor diet can affect our energy levels, so can the intake of toxic substances, whether these be tobacco, alcohol or even carbonated drinks. Most of us keep our intake within reasonable levels, but if things get out of control we are faced not only with depleted energy but also with more serious problems. I remember I was once given a photograph of a young man by his sister, who asked if I could help him. It is possible to connect to someone through a photograph and she was hoping I would be able to send him healing.

As part of the process for distance healing I did a scan of the photograph in my mind, whereby I saw the presence of the young man in my mind's eye. I was shocked to see large holes in the surface of his aura, and asked the woman what was wrong with him. She told me that he was an alcoholic and had also taken drugs. It was my first encounter with addiction as a healer, but since then I have come across this same distressing scenario time and time again.

Addiction often goes hand in hand with mental disturbance, including hallucinations and schizoid behaviour in which the sufferer hears voices. Almost always it is accompanied by depression. Whether the depression comes first I don't know, but it was certainly a factor in all the cases of addiction I have come across.

The majority of situations I deal with involve a friend or relative giving me a photograph of the sufferer and asking for my help. Very rarely do I get approached directly by the sufferer. This means that although I can help, my chances of complete success are limited.

It is essential that the addict has the desire to give up the addiction for him or herself – I can only help alleviate the symptoms, I can't give them the desire. With their aura in tatters, the addict has little chance of a normal life. They will be low in energy because their energy will be seeping away through the gaping holes in their auric field. They are also susceptible to outside influences, as the auric shell or boundary keeps us separate from the spirit world that exists around us – hence the problem with voices and hallucinations.

I am presuming that most people reading this book are not in the depths of a deep depression or complete addicts with uncontrollable cravings. However, any degree of addiction means we are out of control. I personally hate this feeling – it makes me feel weak and I prefer to feel strong. I would therefore strongly recommend that you try to break whatever addictions you have. It will make you feel so empowered. If you find it totally impossible to do this on your own then get professional help.

I used to smoke at least thirty cigarettes every day. I thoroughly enjoyed each and every one of them. I then found that I had developed a little cough, which I didn't think was very attractive. I was single at the time! So I picked a day when I knew I would be moving offices and worked my way down to this 'day of abstinence' by allocating myself fewer cigarettes day by day. By the day of the move I was down to zero.

I also used a mind exercise: every time I wanted a cigarette I imagined one being snuffed out into a bowl of porridge. I cannot stand porridge but I imagined being made to eat the lot! This method worked well for me, and I am still an abstainer twenty years on.

You need to decide your reason for giving up. I chose to give up because it didn't seem very feminine to have a smoker's cough (I'm sorry to say the health reasons didn't have much impression on me at that time). I now have to work on my addiction for chocolate – where's the porridge?

## Loving Others

Once we have re-established a loving relationship with ourselves, we can start to look at our relationships with others. The most important ingredient in any of these relationships is, of course, love.

Every single person on this planet wants happiness and love.

Love is a beautiful word. It conjures up images of light, warmth and security; it brings to mind passion, sex, romance, babies, hugs and cuddles. Wonderful stuff. In this section I'd like to consider the effect love has on our lives and look at ways we can overcome that great barrier to love, which is fear.

Fear is not such a great word – it suggests something dark and foreboding; it conjures up violence, pain and panic. Why would we want these things in our lives when we could have love instead? You might well argue that we don't look for fear and that it is caused by outside forces. You're right, in some cases it is. If you are attacked or your country is at war, you have every reason to be fearful. But millions of people face fear in their lives every single day, fear they have created for themselves.

I would like to introduce you to some ways in which we can move towards a fear-free life – a life filled with love. I have used these methods personally, along with many other normal people who have sought to live a lighter and more easy-going style of life in which *they* are in control and not their fears. We shall also be looking at ways we can use our love and the boundless supply of love in the universe to help others.

I'd like to begin by defining the different kinds of love as I see them. Unfortunately, the English language is a little limited in its range of expressions for the various types – whereas the French seem to have so many more – I guess they have made a study of it!

## Falling in love

I suppose the most exciting form of love is the love we feel when we 'fall in love', which is similar to an addiction. This kind of love is passionate, all consuming and usually leads to sex and wonderful feelings of uniting and becoming immersed in another person. It is strong, wilful and sometimes it takes us where we don't want to go. It burns like a flame that can seem out of control. In fact, when we are in the first throes of being in love we are often out of control. It's a wonderful feeling and has been the basis of many wonderful poems, songs and great music. Sexual love takes us to our greatest heights but, unfortunately, it can also take us to our lowest depths.

When sexual love passes it leaves behind heartbreak and devastation. I can remember the first boy who jilted me. I was completely devastated: I ran home crying and threw myself on my bed in floods of tears. I thought my mother was incredibly callous when she said there would be many more. How could she say such things, I thought – my life was over! Just thinking about it makes me feel pained, even now. However, the bookshops are already full of many marvellous books which set out the course of 'in love' love. I shall back off now and leave Dame Barbara Cartland to reign supreme in this arena.

## Parental love

Let's look at another form of love: the love of a mother for her child. The love of parents for their children is intense and magnificent. Like sexual love, it can be totally consuming. It is about caring and tenderness. It brings us joy, as we see our babies growing and developing. We feel part of their lives as our own and take pride in their achievements.

Parental love is not as overwhelming as being 'in love'; we can live with it from day to day without being burnt up or feeling out of control. But with this type of love come feelings of protection and responsibility. This is where the pain can come in. As our children grow and need our protection less and less, they no longer listen to our guidance as they find their own way, and we can feel the pain of rejection. If we are not careful, the love we have for our children can be possessive.

There is a fine line between being caring and responsible and feeling like we own someone. We have all come across the mother who demands a weekly visit even when her children have grown. We have seen the competitiveness between mother and daughter-in-law. Most of us know what it is like to have to make duty phone calls and duty visits to keep mother or father happy.

Some parents live their lives through their children. They try to compensate for their own lack, or the feelings of inadequacy that they may have. I remember a mother bringing her daughter to me when I lived in Hong Kong. 'Please talk to her,' she said. 'She won't work at school. I want her to be a doctor but she neglects her studies.'

I asked the mother to leave us and talked to this delightful girl for a while. It became clear that she was not very academic and had no interest in school. I wish I could say that she wanted to be an artist or something glamorous but she had no great aspirations. She was being made very unhappy by the constant pressure her mother was putting on her. She was shy and developing eczema, which is a sign of lack of self-esteem. Poor girl.

I gave the girl some healing and gently told her to be herself, and to love herself as she was. I told her to decide for herself what she wanted to be in life and to develop aspirations of her own. It was a difficult case as the mother was strong and overbearing, and I don't doubt the poor girl has continued to have a hard time of it.

Another mother asked me to send healing to her sons. Through the healing she wanted me to make them work harder. She told me that they were not studying and that they had to pass their legal exams if they were to become lawyers. I had the distinct impression that it was only their mother who wanted them to be lawyers and that they were being pushed into this profession against their wishes – hence the lack of diligence in their studies. Poor chaps: I had this mental picture of them being beaten daily by a tyrannical mother until they passed their exams. Actually she was a very nice woman and of course she didn't beat them. She pushed them constantly because she loved them. But I'm sure they felt that their spirit was being beaten.

## Giving and receiving love from your parents

As I have said, many of us go through life looking for confirmation that our parents love us. In some cases we never receive it – even though our parents may love us they may have a problem expressing it.

People will take completely inappropriate careers simply to please their parents. They will fawn, ingratiate themselves and do everything in their power to gain parental love, and if their parents are incapable of giving or showing love they can end up very disappointed and often heartbroken by this lack in their lives.

Do you seek affirmations of love from your parents? Do you find they are not forthcoming? If so, I suggest you learn to accept that your parents have a problem. Look back into their childhoods and see whether they themselves were brought up in a family that expressed love. You could also try writing to them and telling them that you would appreciate some recognition; they might be encouraged to write back and say in a letter what they cannot tell you face to face.

Your parents will always appreciate your love. Everyone enjoys being loved, but especially by their children. The only time I have seen my husband really upset has been during disputes with his children. Fortunately, there have been very few of these and like most families we soon 'kiss and make up' our differences. The occasional phone call or card can transform an aged parent's day so don't be stingy with your expressions of love and care. The worst thing of all is to lose a parent and realise too late that you never properly told them that you loved them.

## Loving friendships

As an only child I found that if I wanted the company of my own generation I had to go out and make friends. It was a great skill to learn and consequently I have an amazing and wonderful collection of friends scattered all around the world. My friends have helped me when I have been down, supported me when I have been unsure, and have shared my happiness.

Someone once said that your family are given and your friends are your choice. I think good friendships are great treasures and they are worth working on. Yes, you do have to work at friendship. You need to show your love to your friends just as you do your family. You need to make the occasional phone call and contact to ensure that your friendships flourish. That said, I find that even when I haven't seen one of my friends for a couple of years, when we get together it's as if we were never apart.

Why don't you put a note to ring one of your friends at the top of your to-do list right now? If you make the effort to ring someone just to tell them how much you appreciate them, I guarantee you it will make you both feel great.

## Love for our partners

What about the love we feel for our partners? You may think this is the truest form of love, that it is pure and abiding. However, even very loving relationships can suffer from unnecessary controlling. Walk around a supermarket or department store on a Saturday and listen: 'Hurry up!', 'Why didn't you do this, why don't you do that?', 'Don't be late', 'Why did you wear those trousers today when you know they don't fit you?', 'I like this so why don't you?', etc. Nag, nag, nag, woman to man, man to woman. Wonderful love!

Do you ever feel embarrassed by your partner during social occasions? Do you ever wish they wouldn't have that last drink? Please, God, don't let them tell that joke again? Why does everyone else's husband seem such a laugh when they're being over the top, but your own husband a total embarrassment? Control, control, control.

When will we realise that we are not responsible for anyone else but ourselves? What does it matter if my husband makes a total idiot of himself? It's himself he is showing up, not me. Anyway who is to judge? Everyone else is laughing and enjoying themselves so he can't be doing it all wrong. Why do I feel so flushed and uncomfortable then?

The answer is that we take responsibility for the people that are near us and we like to make them fit our standards, our idea of how we think they should be. We try to change people. We meet them, fall in love with them and then try to change them. What's wrong with accepting them as they are, with taking them warts and all and loving the total package? Why not take both the good and the so-called bad and leave behind the fault-finding and point scoring? Accept, don't judge. Ah, now we are coming closer to the true meaning of the word love as I see it.

## Unconditional love

The love that I want us to fill our days with, and be our predominant emotion, is unconditional love. The definitions of unconditional love are set out below.

Unconditional love is loving:
- Without judgement.
- Without controlling.
- Without possessing.
- Without demands.

Unconditional love is:
- Total acceptance.
- Care.
- Patience.
- Respect.
- Tenderness.
- Compassion.
- Kindness.

Unconditional love is the greatest gift you can give to anyone, including yourself.

EXERCISE: LOVING UNCONDITIONALLY

- Turn off the phones, find a quiet room and close the door.
- Close your eyes and breathe in deeply four times. As you breathe in, feel gentle waves of light surround you. Feel peace and calm. As you breathe out, imagine that all your troubles and cares are leaving you.
- Take yourself somewhere you love: your imaginary garden, a beach, a wood, a hilltop.
- Sit for a while and contemplate the people in your life that you love.
- See these people walk up to you and consider how you love each of them in turn. Take your time over this exercise – it can change your relationships for ever.
- If you feel that you control, possess or judge the person in any way, make a promise to be unconditional in your love for them from now on.
- If it feels right, put your arms around the person and feel the strength of this new, undemanding love – feel how sweet it is.
- When you have spent time with each person, come back into the room, bringing your unconditional love with you, and start practising it from this moment on.

---

There are many words for love, including kindness, compassion, respect, caring, acceptance, understanding, forgiveness and tolerance.

---

You never know what is behind the façade a person puts up – someone may be mean but do you know what meanness they have suffered at the hands of someone else? Someone may be abusive but perhaps this is to cover the pain of abuse they have themselves received. If someone has difficulty loving then it may be that they have never been loved. These are not excuses but reasons.

I can hear you saying 'That's all very well but what about the rest of us? How can we get behind the façade and get people to love us in the way we feel they should?' The answer is that it is difficult and takes time. But remember the power of the energy you emit: the law of cause and effect. What you give out you get back, and that comes into play here. There is no doubt that if you give out pure, unconditional love you will get back the same in return. It may take time and it may be that the love you get back comes from a different source. Your aged aunt may never change, for example, but you will meet new people who think the same way as you. You may even find that your aunt *will* change!

Sometimes people treat us in a certain way because of the way we treat them. I have found this myself: when I stop nagging my husband, he treats me much better. Nagging and controlling are catching. If you push someone they have to resist in some way. Try it out for yourself. Don't expect instant change but watch over a period of weeks the difference in those close to you. Have patience. You will be amazed.

---

**Remember that you can only change yourself. You are only responsible for yourself and you can only work on yourself. The changes in your attitude and energies will affect others.**

---

So we have now connected with our inner selves and brought love back into our lives. Our next step is to look more closely at our relationships – letting go those that harm us and finding ways that we can improve those that we wish to keep active and healthy.

# 5

# Creating Loving Relationships

In this chapter, we look at the powerful process of cutting the etheric cords – the energy streams – that hold us to relationships or aspects of a relationship that no longer benefit us. We consider some of the common problems in relationships that take us away from true love, and find ways to break destructive patterns. Are there other attachments in your life that you can't let go? We look at the pain of bereavement, and the attachments we have to our material possessions.

Once you have gained greater respect and love for yourself, you will find it reflected in your new relationships. It will show itself in the friends you attract and the potential partners that come into your life. However, you may find that you are still bound by the past.

When a relationship has ended, it is not always easy to let it go completely. It can be particularly difficult when someone has left us. We may still love them and yearn for their company and presence. We may also be bound by fear. We may be afraid to let go a relationship that is hurting us emotionally or even physically. We could be fearful of being alone; we may fear the loss of security that a partnership offers us.

Holding on to the past makes it very difficult for us to move on and make new liaisons. We need to let it go once it no longer serves us, and free ourselves so that the space left in our lives can be filled by someone better suited to share our journey. We need someone to enjoy the fun of life with us and someone who will comfort us in our darker moments.

Everyone is looking for someone special and the past can often act as an obstacle in our search. Let's think about why it is so difficult to forget someone who has been close to us in the past.

## Relationships and the Cords that Bind

If you have a close relationship with someone you create an energy cord between yourself and that person, engendered by the constant stream of strong emotional thoughts you are sending out to each other.

An energy cord is similar to a thought form but it has the appearance of an old-fashioned pyjama cord, or the cord you use to tie back curtains: two thick threads that twist around each other as the relationship grows. We call these 'etheric cords' and they link the two people concerned between the chakras of the heart or solar plexus (we looked at these input output energy points on pages 24–5).

Lovers' cords will grow between the heart chakras, the energy centres found in the centre of the chest that relate to the giving and receiving of love. Other cords of attachment are more likely to connect at the solar plexus, the chakra above the navel that is associated with emotions and willpower.

The length of the relationship and the intensity of the emotions involved will affect the cord's strength: the more in love a couple are the stronger their cord. So long-term lovers are likely to have strong cords; the intensity of their love and passion will be reflected in the cord's brightness.

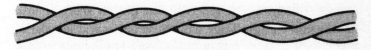

*The Etheric Cords*

The breaking or untwining of a cord can cause severe pain, feelings of loss and heartache. A couple who have been married all their adult life will be completely 'attached' to each other and the loss of one or the other will not only cause severe pain in the heart, but will also leave the survivor feeling as if half of them is missing. This is because their auras will have totally intermingled and they will be feeling the loss of half of their energy field as well as the pain of the severed etheric cord.

The expression 'heart strings' has been used by songwriters and poets for hundreds of years to describe the cords of love between lovers. It's a wonderful analogy. However, if the relationship ends in separation, the partner that leaves will sever their cord, leaving the one who is abandoned with a broken heart. It is not the physical heart that is broken but the heart chakra, which is damaged when the person leaving 'pulls back' their cord.

The pain is real and it can take at least a year for the wound and the deep pain to heal.

Apart from being a passageway for love, the cords can be a source of energy for those connected. If the relationship is balanced then both partners benefit from this connection and it will be a great source of comfort and support. In most relationships there are times when either one or the other person will need more help and love. If one partner feels down or depressed, the cord will ensure that they have a constant feeling of being wanted and loved. But if the relationship becomes one-sided, one person will always be receiving the greater share of love, caring and energy. They will get stronger and less caring while their partner becomes depleted and begins to lose self-esteem.

---

If we pass our hurt to our nearest and dearest and in doing so hurt them, we destroy their love – the very thing that can relieve our pain.

---

## Losing that first bloom of love

As we gradually get to know someone we have fallen in love with, the first bloom of love tends to fade. What happens to that wonderful feeling of being in love, that completely non-judgemental attitude we felt towards our lover? Why do we see couples arguing and sniping when a few years or even months before they were looking dewy-eyed at each other?

You could say that reality steps in as the passion fades. This seems a shame and it surely isn't necessary for our relationships to go downhill so drastically. We are both the same people so why should our perception of each other change so much? It may be that we only fall in love with the veneer of our partner and when we look deeper we find many things that don't sit so well with us. Or maybe we put on an act when we first meet someone and only let our true selves come through afterwards.

## Common relationship problems and cutting the cords

I want us to look at some of the reasons why relationships start to suffer and consider what we can do to counteract this. Fortunately, we can often retrieve our original state of love by cutting the cords of a relationship – I shall show you how very soon – and letting go those aspects that are causing the rift.

### Possessiveness and jealousy

One of the primary causes of turbulence in romantic relationships is possessiveness, and its counterpart emotion of jealousy. By being possessive you can destroy a beautiful association and drive a person from your life.

The Arabs have a saying: 'Grasp sand in a tight fist and it runs from the side; hold sand in a cupped hand and it will stay.' No one likes to feel bound and held down by even the most loving person; the natural reaction is to flee. By cutting the cords of a possessive relationship we can be free to enjoy a natural and loving one – with the same person if we wish. Jealousy is destructive for both parties. At the root of most possessiveness and jealousy is a fear of rejection and abandonment.

If you are a jealous person, examine the underlying emotion – is it fear of being left? Does your partner deliberately make you feel insecure? Do they abuse you emotionally by creating a feeling of insecurity in you? Does your partner treat you as a possession? Do you treat your partner as a possession? If you have answered yes to any of these, you may need to cut the cords that bind you together and either move on or re-establish a more loving and unfettered approach to your partnership.

### Dependency

When we lean too much on another person we become a burden that they have to carry around. Have you ever given someone your arm and felt that you were literally carrying them because they let you take all their weight? It is difficult to take responsibility for another. I'm not talking about the times we look after those who are close to us when they are ill. I am talking about the dependency that develops when one person leans on another and leaves them to make all the decisions and choices.

Needy people tend to look to another person not only to fulfil their needs but also to take full responsibility for them. Check that you don't lean on your friends, parents or partner in this way. Do you rely on them too much? Do you ask them to make your decisions for you? Alternatively, do members of your family, your friends or your partner lean too much on you?

### Controlling and nagging

Everyone has the right to be their own person and live their life the way they wish. I believe that even when we think it's for a person's greater good, we should avoid nagging and controlling.

Let people make their own way and be free to do what they wish. You can tell them you are unhappy about behaviour that affects you – and if they continually upset you, ask yourself if they are doing it deliberately and, if so, why. But if someone's behaviour doesn't affect you really and truly, why try to make them change? We have no right to control another person. If you sometimes find yourself trying to change your partner, think about cutting the controlling cord and replacing it with a cord of unconditional love.

Before suggesting to anyone else that they cut their cords, I felt I should do so in my own relationship with my husband. I had a tendency to believe I knew what was best for him, and I wanted to stop my nagging – so one night while he was sleeping I cut the cord. I must admit I was a little worried that he might wake up and pack his bag! But no, quite the opposite. The next morning, before he was truly awake, he turned to me, put his arms around me and said, 'Do you know how very much I love you?' It was great confirmation of a very powerful process that has helped many people to recondition their partnerships.

Josephine was having a problem with her boyfriend. He would seem really keen but as soon as she showed any signs of wanting to get closer he backed off. When she came to one of my workshops, he hadn't called her for weeks so she decided to let him go.

The cords are released in two stages: first we let go the emotions associated with a relationship – all the jealousy, controlling, dominance, possessiveness, etc. – then we actually break the cord. In the tea break between the two stages, Josephine turned on her mobile phone so she could ring to check on her young children at home. The phone rang immediately. It was the man she had just released. He hadn't been in touch for weeks, yet here he was calling her. He told her that he had a great urge to see her and said he had her so clearly in his mind he wanted to drive up to see her that night. This meant a four-hour car journey!

Josephine was delighted and couldn't believe how quickly the exercise had worked. They sat up all night and re-established the basis of their relationship. When I saw her last it was still going strong, although now as a great and abiding friendship.

We can use the cord-cutting exercise not only to let go yesterday's relationships but also to improve our current ones. Let's look at some of the reasons you might decide to break the cord that connects you to someone:

- They have a strong undesirable influence over you.
- They are trying to control or dominate you.
- You still love them but they don't love you.
- They are unobtainable and your emotional bond to them is ruining your life.
- You have a passionate relationship, but you are not as compatible on an everyday level.
- You are trying to control, dominate or change someone.
- You wish to be more independent.

Before you embark on this exercise, make sure you are aware of the power of the process. You will be disconnecting and it may leave you feeling a little empty – especially if you have had the attachment for some time. However, we shall be replacing the cord of attachment with a cord of LOVE so don't fear that the other person involved will no longer love you – they may well love you more.

EXERCISE: CUT YOUR CORDS

**Stage 1**

- Find a quiet place and sit down with paper and pen.
- Take a moment or two to think quietly about the relationships or attachments that you wish to release or change in your life.
- Write down a few lines about each relationship or aspect of a relationship that you wish to let go.
- Burn the paper and as you do so let the emotions attached to the relationship go for ever.

**Stage 2**

- Close your eyes and relax, breathing in deeply four times.
- Let your roots grow deep into the ground and feel the strong connection with the earth beneath you.
- See yourself entering a beautiful garden which is filled with your favourite flowers. Walk around the garden and take time to feel its peace and tranquillity.
- Walk on deeper and deeper into the garden to its centre, where you find a rose garden. In this delightful and totally secluded sanctuary you see a bench. Notice a pair of golden scissors lying on the bench. Walk over to the bench and sit down.
- Think of the cords that you wish to let go one by one. When you have a cord in your mind's eye, take the scissors and cut through it. Let the relationships go with love, using the release symbol (*see pages 111–2*) to help you.
- When you have released all the cords, think of each person you have released yourself from in turn, and visualise a new, strong pink cord linking you to that

person. This cord represents unconditional, undemanding, non-judgemental love.

- See a ball of golden light fill your heart centre and
  your solar plexus and feel it healing any sense of loss
  you may have.

- Sit quietly for a while and determine that in future
  your relationships will be filled with love and
  harmony, balance and trust.

- When you are ready, come back into the room and
  bring that determination with you.

---

## Past life connections

Through the process of healing I have learned that we
live through many lifetimes. We return in many guises
but our soul – that part of us that is permanent and
continuing – survives death and comes back again. This
process is called reincarnation and it is a central tenet of
many cultures and religions (I shall be looking at reincarnation in more detail in chapter six). It is my belief
that we often connect to people who we have known in
previous lives. This can sometimes cause problems – we
may not be able to make things work with a partner, for
example, but nevertheless be strongly attached to them
because we have known them in a past life.

I experienced this with my first husband. We loved
each other deeply but we were more like brother and
sister than husband and wife. I realise now that our bond
was based on previous life experiences, and that our
present-day characters were not suited in marriage. Once
we split up, we found we were the very best of friends –
we would still be great friends today if our current partners could have coped with it! This next case study shows

what can happen when we are pulled together by these old soul connections.

This is a rather unusual story but I have included it to show the power the past has to affect us and also the power we have to let it go.

Pamela had an unusual problem: her current relationship was based on an overwhelming sexual drive that drew her and her partner together with an amazing and insatiable force! This would have been wonderful, but they were not as compatible in many other areas. He was a very religious man and kept himself apart from earthly affairs and material matters. He wanted to live a simple and quiet life. She, on the other hand, was vivacious and fun and enjoyed a fuller and more upbeat lifestyle – in other words, she liked to party! She was also extremely spiritual, but believed that we are here to live our lives to the full and to enjoy ourselves on our route through.

Pamela's incompatibility with her partner was causing her frustration and concern. She felt locked in by the sexual force that was bonding them together. She was convinced it was a karmic connection and that they had lived together in past lives. However, she was prepared to sacrifice the relationship rather than let it continue as it was.

Before we cleared the cords I did a scan of the woman's past and saw two lives flicker past me. In the first, I saw her current partner as a priest. He was totally besotted by my patient, who in this past life appeared as a harlot and was teasing and taunting the priest with her sexuality. The priest could not restrain himself and had a tumultuous affair with her. His involvement caused him great torment on account of his deep religious beliefs and his vow of celibacy.

In the second lifetime I saw a similar scenario but this time the woman's partner was a monk and he ended the relationship by strangling her! No wonder she felt so strongly drawn to the man. (I should stress that she is by no means a harlot in this lifetime!)

When we came to the cord releasing exercise I saw a whole bundle of cords that were totally entwined. My patient tried pulling them apart but in the end she resorted to cutting. It was hard going but eventually most of the cords were disconnected. There were just three left, one of which was black. This black cord was the most difficult to break and I believe it was the one that linked to the episode where she had been killed by her partner in her past life. When it finally broke we both felt a huge release of energy.

It left my patient feeling quite weak and she required some healing on her heart and solar plexus chakras.

## Achieving Better Relationships

As well as untangling our cords we need to untangle our thought processes. We need to take responsibility for future involvements and our attitudes to those close to us. You are the only person who can change your inter-personal behaviour patterns and all I can do is give you some ideas that may help you. Needy people are vulner-able. Be strong and fill your own life and don't look to others to fill the gaps for you.

## Be independent

If you are a fully independent person with your own thoughts, your own ideas and a full and interesting life, you are less likely to need to lean on another person – as soon as you start to lean you become dependent. Dependency leads to vulnerability and even the kindest person in the world is going to find that irritating. If your partner has a touch of the bully in them it will bring out the worst in them.

Strength comes from being independent and having a full life. Fill your spare time with things that interest you, and don't rely entirely on your partner to entertain you. Personally, if someone leans on me I feel the burden intensely and I am smothered by it – I'm filled with a desire to move away. I am sure you also know this feeling, so try not to lean on other people too much. You may find they reject you even though they have good feelings for you, simply because they cannot bear to be over-whelmed.

## Support your partner

A relationship should be a mutually supportive system where each helps the other when they are in need. If one person is forever leaning on the other, both will fall down. Whereas if both of you see yourself as a support for the other, you will create a beautiful harmony in your rela-tionship.

This is something you often see with older couples, who look out for each other's interests in a mutually caring and supportive way, and have stopped fussing over the differences between them.

We can show our support in many small ways in our

daily life. I personally love those short phone calls from my husband in which he asks me how my day is going; they are like little signals of his support and love. Other ways we can show our support is by taking our partner's side when they are being attacked verbally by others, or by showing confidence in their abilities, especially when they are going through difficulties at work.

Couples often argue the most when they hit trouble in their lives. This is precisely the time when each needs the support of the other.

Sometimes just thinking about the other person can take away some of the immediacy of the hurt or fear that you are both suffering. The challenges that your shared lives bring are opportunities for you to dig deep into yourself for compassion and love. You can often turn the worst circumstances into opportunities to bond more deeply with one another.

## Love rather than possess

There is a huge difference between loving and possessing, but some people get into the habit of thinking that they own their partners – treating them as someone to take around with them and use. Check your own relationship. If you truly love someone you will be prepared to let them go, if it is for their highest good. Letting them go completely is, of course, the last resort and I doubt many of us would want to put it into practice. However, you may need reminding that your partner is an individual, who has the right to their own preferences and decisions about what they do with their time and where they want to be.

Time apart often brings you closer and makes the time you spend together more refreshing and interesting. It's not a bad thing to develop separate hobbies and pastimes, and it can mean you have more to talk about when you do get together.

## Care rather than control

In a close relationship, whether between mother and daughter, father and son, brother and sister, employer and employee or between lovers, we need to be on the alert for controlling habits.

If you impose your ideas and tastes on another person you are trying to control them. If you think you know better and regularly pass on your comments about health, education, dress sense, social behaviour and drinking levels, then you will know what I am talking about. There is a huge difference between being caring and being controlling.

When you care you nurture and cherish; you do little things to please the other person. You show care by nursing them when they are sick and down. You don't tell them continuously what they are doing wrong. Remember that you are only responsible for yourself and you can only change yourself. We are all responsible for our own health, our own spiritual progress and what ultimately happens to us.

**If your caring is abused then consider whether the relationship is beneficial to you.**

## Breaking Destructive Patterns

There is nothing so energy depleting and self-destructive as an abusive relationship. It is the complete antithesis of balance. When one person is completely dominated by another then there is little chance for personal growth and little chance for happiness.

Do you seem to attract abusive relationships, whether they be with friends, partners or work colleagues? Do you find that people dominate you and mentally or physically abuse you? Do you find that the same unfortunate experiences keep repeating in your life? Do you find yourself drawn to the same type of unsuitable partner again and again?

We can easily find ourselves caught in a loop of repeated circumstances if we continue to hold the same attitudes and views. It isn't easy to change but the first step towards change is to acknowledge that it is yourself that is attracting these situations and that you are not 'unlucky'.

As well as unsuitable partners, we can also find ourselves repeatedly attracting negative situations in our lives. Do you ever hear yourself saying 'just my luck', 'it always happens to me', 'I can't believe this is happening again' – as you get made redundant for the third time, or another man has been unfaithful, or you have crashed your car for the fourth time in a year?

If you have any such thoughts then the chances are you are caught up in a loop of negativity and have created a pattern for yourself. Our old friend the law of cause and effect is operational here – if you give out negative energy vibrations (bad vibes) then you will attract negative situations – FACT. There is no disputing this; it is universal law and as such is immutable.

These situations and relationships bring with them depression, anxiety, low self-esteem and all the negative emotions that we are trying to let go in our lives. Life becomes a battle when you surround yourself with people and situations that are not in the state of peace, love and strength which you are trying to attain.

Fortunately, the causal law can work for us as well as against us. If you give out positive vibes then you will attract the good things in life like success and good relationships, love and happiness. But before you can do this you may need some help to break the pattern and loop in which you are caught.

To break away from negative thought patterns and situations, you need first to acknowledge what it is that keeps recurring in your life that you wish to let go. Just by making this acknowledgement you will put yourself on the right track and the changes will begin. Follow this simple mind exercise and you will be amazed by what a kick-start it gives you by releasing you from the bonds of your old situations.

---

EXERCISE: BREAK YOUR PATTERNS

- Find a place of peace and calm where you won't be disturbed by phones, children, pets, partners or anything else.
- Breathe in deeply four times.
- Imagine you have roots growing out of your feet down into the ground, connecting you to the Earth and keeping you secure.
- Visualise yourself in a favourite place, like a garden or a beach, where you can be totally alone.
- See a large piece of wood and a small knife in front of you.

- Take the knife and spell out in the wood whatever negative pattern you are planning to break – for example: 'over-critical of myself', 'dominating', 'selfish', 'allowing myself to be dominated'.

- Now pick up an axe that you see lying beside the wooden block and break up the words, the pattern, with all your strength. As you do this know that you are destroying that mind-set for ever.

- Finally see a bonfire blazing in front of you, and throw the piece of wood into it. Watch the flames turn your old pattern into light as your negative pattern is reversed.

- Slowly come back into your surroundings, knowing that the burden of your negativity has been lifted from you.

## Letting Go of People who Have Died

I am often asked whether one should cut the cords of a relationship when a person has died. This is an extremely emotive subject, and yet I believe that if you have found it difficult to let someone go after their passing, it can serve you and them well to cut the cords between you. I should stress that this is a personal choice, but if you feel it would help you, by all means go ahead. Remember that it will never destroy the love you have for that person, but it may help you move on in your life.

Personally, I do not believe that death is a termination. I see it as a transition from one life to another. I believe that when we die our soul moves into another dimension of existence and another vibration of energy. In that other realm, which we commonly refer to as the astral plane, the newly arrived soul is met and comforted by other members of their family and friends who have already died. I have seen many souls enjoying rapturous welcomes amid much jollity and celebration.

If a person is traumatised by their death experience they are led to a quiet and peaceful place of healing. Their journey is a positive and uplifting experience in every respect. The new reality of the astral plane seems to reflect the wishes and dreams of a person's soul – so an Englishman might arrive at a place of pastoral beauty with rolling hills and a sunny aspect (a great chance to engineer the weather conditions); an Arab might choose an oasis in the desert. Your soul stays in this state for as long as you need, and then you move on to more evolved ways of being, in which you don't need the comfort of your last life's visual memories around you. We shall take a deeper look at this interim state in chapter eight.

## Coping with loss

Even if we believe that all will be well for the person who is passing on, there is inevitably a great deal of pain and suffering for those left behind. We are not very good at grieving in the West. I have been to funerals where the chief mourners stood rigid and tight-lipped throughout – doing their utmost not to reveal any of their deep and painful feelings. We create so many problems for ourselves by doing this.

In the East, on the other hand, funeral mourners are encouraged to wail, cry and generally let out their emotions. Sometimes they seem to go a little too far – I guess by our standards anyway – throwing themselves prostrate on the body of the departed and falling into trances. However, I truly believe that it is not a sign of weakness to show grief in public.

We also need to give ourselves time to get over the loss of someone close. As anyone knows who has been through this, it takes a good year before you can even see life in any normal light. You have to expect this – if we were given permission to shut ourselves away and lick our wounds in the way that animals do, I am sure we would be better for it. In my opinion, we try to force grieving people back into 'normality' far too soon. We also have a habit of avoiding people who are mourning, or at least avoiding their grief.

I know how much I wanted to talk about my father after he died. I wanted to say how much I still loved him, but I didn't because I didn't want to upset other people. I also really appreciated every kindness, every card and every loving thought sent my way. Don't forget either that crying is the most natural way for us to let go those unwanted emotions; shedding tears is a wonderfully cleansing process for both men and women.

## What Else do We Attach to?

Sai Baba, the great Indian spiritual leader and teacher, once said that all suffering comes from attachments. It is our feelings of possession for people and things that cause us the pain of loss and hurt when they are taken from us. In fact, none of our possessions can truly be called our own. Once we die we cannot take any of them with us, and therefore we should consider them as loans rather than permanently ours.

When we lose a piece of jewellery, for example, especially a piece of sentimental value, we are often devastated. But if we had been told when we were given it that it would be leaving us in two years' time and moving on to someone else, we would be far less upset when it actually left us, because we wouldn't feel that our ownership was permanent.

For your own benefit, I strongly advise you not to get too attached to things. Don't hanker after things from your past. Remember them as an experience that was wonderful and appreciate the sentiments that came with the gift – those memories can never be taken away. I once lost a ring that my father gave me for my twenty-first birthday. It was a very sad loss, but I remind myself that the love with which he gave me the ring will be with me for ever.

Another painful source of attachment is homesickness. As an expatriate myself, I have met many people who find it very difficult to be away from their home country. The problem is partly the attachment they want to maintain. The most successful expatriates are those that realise the benefits of their new home and so fill their lives. These people live in the moment and extract all the joy they can from the experience of living in a new culture and meeting new people.

If you have to move homes often, you also learn to let go some of your possessions, simply because it would be too difficult to take them with you. I confess I am a bit of a squirrel but I feel so much lighter once I've been through the cupboards and thrown away the things I no longer need or passed them on to the nearest charity shop.

Have a look in your cupboards today and see if there are any items of clothing or household utensils that you haven't used for two years. If you haven't found a use for them in that time the chances are you won't need them in the future, so let them go. Clearing the cupboards is great exercise and it's a powerful symbolic process – it's

a way of telling ourselves that we are living in the present
and not the past.

---

**Kindness is the most effective destroyer of barriers
between individuals and nations.**

---

## Choosing Your Future Relationships

Who you spend your daily life with is tremendously
important to your wellbeing. So once you have determined to break with non-supportive and destructive relationships, you need to think about how you are going to
choose who you spend your time with in future.

Firstly, I would suggest that you don't look for a
partner until you are happy and content with yourself. If
you try to find a partner when you are needy you are
going to be looking for someone to make you happy.
Happiness comes from within and to ask someone else
to make you happy is a tremendously high order.

Neither do you want the responsibility of making
someone else happy. Love and care for someone, yes, but
don't be entirely responsible for their happiness. How
can you be? How can you know what will truly please
someone? Look for peace of mind for yourself first –
then, when you have worked through your issues, your
problems, your fears, find someone with whom you feel
comfortable and who attracts you. Listen to your heart
not your head when making your choice. It's not a logical
exercise so feel it, don't think it!

Of course, you won't find the perfect mate – there is
no such thing. If a person were perfect then they'd be

playing a harp. Try to view your partner as a whole and accept the total package. Don't rely on other people's opinions, but listen to what you feel. A lot of our judgements are impressed upon us by society and convention.

Looking at my own marriage, I would say that, generally speaking, my husband is the perfect mate for me – but he does like going to seedy bars from time to time, and then gets home late and somewhat intoxicated. Most of my friends find it amazing that I don't get into a tizzy about this behaviour. In fact, I rarely say anything to him about it. Why should I? He enjoys it, it doesn't hurt me, he doesn't drag me around those places and it doesn't happen very often.

If I were to let the concerns of others guide me I would be throwing saucepans at his head when he comes home like this and crying into my pillow – or throwing that at him as well! I don't see it that way. As a result he thinks he is incredibly lucky to have such a tolerant wife and I guess he loves me even more for that. So listen to your own inner feelings and be your own master.

# 6

# Forgiveness and Clearing Your Karma

When we learn to forgive ourselves and others we can step on to the pathway to happiness and true healing. Forgiveness clears the way for the release of our karma. In this chapter, we let go pain and guilt by learning how to forgive. Do bad things keep happening to you? We consider the reasons behind negative events and situations by exploring the spiritual law of cause and effect. If you push the pendulum one way, whether in this life or a past one, karma dictates that it has to swing back.

Now that we have let go the past and revalued our relationships, we can make the final steps to our complete healing. No doubt you have come up against the 'onion syndrome' I referred to at the beginning of the book – as you heal one layer of your problems, so another layer is revealed with all its attendant issues.

You will probably need to continue your self-healing work for a long time, but as each layer is healed so you will feel stronger and lighter. In this chapter, I would like to move on to what I consider is the most powerful of all healing processes – forgiveness. Forgiveness takes courage and strength but it is mightily powerful and will help you to heal in an amazing way.

---

Most acts of cruelty are the result of inner pain. Focus on that pain and try your best to forgive, realising the suffering this pain has caused both the giver and the receiver.

---

## *Forgiving Others*

Forgiveness is an action as well as a state of mind. The act of forgiveness is a difficult one as it takes you deep inside yourself, and accesses the most powerful of emotions. In my opinion, it surpasses any act of love, because it takes us from one polarity to another – from the most negative place to the most positive.

I see Jesus's forgiveness of those who murdered him as the outstanding act of his life. His attitude and the compassion he felt towards those who had betrayed him and physically hurt him so badly make him a great role model. The act of forgiveness frees and releases not only ourselves, but also the person we forgive, by assuaging their burden of guilt.

A young Indian woman came to me one day asking for my help. Her problem was her sister-in-law – she hated her. At first, I found this difficult to believe as, as far as I could see, my patient had a very mild and easy-going nature. However, as she told me her tale I could feel her deep dislike for the other women coming through in her voice.

As an Indian, the woman believed very strongly in the unity of family, and the duty of each family member to help one another. She believed that both she and her sister-in-law (who was also Indian) should respect her parents and visit them regularly, so that they could share time and love with their children and grandchildren. This is the conventional Indian attitude towards family life.

My patient explained that she had been distraught when her brother married because he had chosen a wife who didn't follow the family mores and who actively discouraged her husband from visiting the rest of the family, particularly his parents. Her sister-in-law also spoke badly about the rest of the family when alone with him, and had apparently created a great rift in family relations.

Of course, I can only tell my patient's side of the story but, in fact, that doesn't matter – however it had come about, this was how my patient perceived her sister-in-law's behaviour and this was what had caused her to hate her so much. She said that her feelings had become like a poison inside her. Whenever she thought of her sister-in-law she felt weak with hatred and anger. It was making her ill and yet she couldn't let the feelings go. As a spiritual person she was well aware of the damage these attitudes were causing her at every level.

The hatred my patient felt had become like an addiction – she couldn't imagine living without it, yet she wanted to be rid of it. The core of her problem seemed to be the slight that she felt this woman's actions were on her parents. Shame is a very powerful emotion in Eastern culture and she believed that her parents were being shamed by this woman's treatment of them.

I asked the woman to look at the problem from a different perspective, and to recognise that she was behaving as if she were responsible for her parents and what was happening to them. This, of course, is not a viable position.

I then asked her to try to step back from the emotion of it all: to think of the woman objectively and consider why she was being so isolationist. It could be that her sister-in-law had problems of her own. Maybe she was frightened or intimidated by her in-laws in some way. I asked her to stand aside from her hatred and see it as a being on its own that had invaded her, to see it as something to reject and release.

We carried on talking for some time and then I talked my patient through a full release of her feelings. She saw them leave her body as a dark cloud and transmute into golden light as they reached the Sun. The process brought forth many tears. She told me later that she spent the rest of the day being sick and knew that the poison of the hatred had finally left her body. Afterwards, she found that she could cope far more easily with her sister-in-law – she never managed to like her, but neither did she hate her any more.

There have probably been many people in your life who have upset you or hurt you in some way, whether at work or in your home and family life. It's not unusual to feel resentment and bitterness towards one's parents, for example. It isn't easy to bring up children and many parents seem to make quite a fist of it, judging by the

number of my patients who have experienced difficult
and loveless childhoods. The bitterness often continues
even when the parents have passed on.

Whatever the cause of your anger, hatred or resentment, you need to forgive and let bygones be bygones if
you want peace and happiness in your life now. Let the
past go and treat the present as a gift.

## Why we get hurt

Let us a look now in more detail at what happens when
someone hurts us and why they do it. We may be able
to limit the hurt we feel by taking a different view of the
situation.

Let me give you an everyday example. It's your birthday
coming up and your partner has made no mention of it.
You have a choice – you can either remind them, or you
can create a test to see if they remember! I have tried
both ways. You can guess what happened when I kept
quiet – my husband forgot and I woke up on my birthday
without a present and with a huge feeling of hurt, plenty
of tears and a spoilt day on my hands! On top of which
my husband felt incredibly guilty and, although he did
his best to redress the situation, there was a lot of bad
feeling and unnecessary pain all round.

Personally I find emotional upsets like these exhausting
and nowadays I try to avoid them if at all possible. I
always make sure that my husband is fully aware of all
upcoming birthdays and anniversaries, and I let him
know my expectations so there are no disappointments.
In other words, I don't try to manipulate the situation
and deliberately make him feel guilty.

It is so easy to become 'holier than thou', act the victim,
and use this to gain sympathy and attention. Do you ever

create situations in order to make someone feel guilty? Do you ever deliberately do more than your partner, your family members or your work colleagues in order to make them feel lazy?

It's very easy to fall into this way of behaving and we normally do it to get sympathy or to make ourselves feel better. We may be trying to manipulate someone into being more considerate, more attentive or into fulfilling our wishes. It is not a great way to go – it causes an imbalance in relationships, and the guilt induced in another person can eventually turn to anger, which in turn leads to arguments and bad feelings. If you want to live in harmony try not to put people in a position where they have to ask for forgiveness.

Of course there will also be many occasions where you are the innocent victim of another's anger and pain. However, I truly believe that we bring about most of the events that occur in our lives, and that they are all part of an evolving development process aimed at our greater good.

If anyone were encapsulated in a cocoon of love and safety from childhood to adulthood, they would experience very little and would certainly not learn how to cope with life's challenges.

We may not always understand why things are happening to us – especially those things that are traumatic and upsetting – but as life evolves we can often look back and see the good that has come out of these events.

## Avoiding some of the problems

If we accept the premise that what we give out we receive, and that we are the creators of our own life events, it is possible to see how we might draw situations to us which, on the surface, seem unprovoked. I shall be expanding upon the law of cause and effect later in this chapter, but just for now let's consider why we sometimes attract situations that seem disturbing or negative.

In chapter one we looked at how our thoughts can create illness and disturb our energy flow. If we take this a step further, we will see that disturbed energy actually attracts further disturbed or misaligned energy – because the universal natural law of like attracting like comes into play.

We are most comfortable with people who think as we do and hold the same values, so we gravitate towards people who are similar to ourselves. In the same way, our innermost thoughts send out a stream of energy that is picked up by the inner antennae, or sixth sense of those around us. This means that our inner weaknesses and doubts are projected out to the world and are sometimes picked up and taken advantage of by other people.

We can see this clearly when looking around the school playground. Children who have either an ill-defined sense of identity or who lack self-esteem will often be bullied. The bullies are children who themselves are lacking in some way and who see the shy and nervous child as an easy target. They gain power and raise their own self-esteem by picking on and tormenting the weaker child.

I remember a TV programme I saw a while ago about mugging. The New York police had set up a series of video cameras to monitor an area that had become infamous for the extremely high number of assaults that had taken place there. The police gradually noticed a similarity between the people who became victims, and they also found that these same unfortunate people were being mugged again and again. It seems that they were sending out fear signals with their body language: they kept looking over their shoulders as though they were expecting to be attacked, they had their heads down, their shoulders hunched and their hands either in their pockets or clasped in front of them as though protecting themselves.

Those people who walked confidently and fearlessly through the streets, on the other hand, sent out the message 'don't mess with me' (it was an American programme so please excuse the slang!). I was most impressed by the programme's analysis as it confirmed what I have often thought – we send out messages and therefore in a way create and draw some of these traumas to us.

There are many reasons why we are subjected to traumatic and upsetting situations, many of which are beyond our conscious control. However, if we can do anything to avoid the onset of trouble it is obviously a good idea to do so. Here are a few suggestions that will help you avoid attracting trouble, and so minimise the number of traumatic events and disturbing experiences in your life.

- Avoid dark streets and 'dangerous' locations.
- When walking alone, walk confidently and purposefully. Always have your car keys ready so that you can get into your car quickly if necessary.
- Pay particular attention to your environment when away from home – many people get into trouble when on holiday.
- Try to avoid visualising disturbing events. Whenever you become worried or fearful draw your thoughts to a positive event in your life – the birth of a child or a marriage, for example.
- Avoid over-exposure to violence either in the news or in films. Watching scary movies can encourage a

mind-set of fear. If something dreadful has happened in the world, don't become a news junky and watch the same distressing scenes over and over again. If there is nothing else to watch, turn the television off and play some peaceful music.

• Don't pass on your fears to others or let them pass theirs on to you.

## Understanding why people cause pain

How we handle difficult or unpleasant events can make a big difference to the way they affect us in the short and the long term. We can reduce the emotional pain we feel by looking at things another way and seeking a greater understanding of the person who has done the harm.

Why do people hurt others? Why would someone be deliberately cruel to another human being or animal? What good does it do them and how can they live with themselves afterwards? I find it difficult to come to terms with some people's behaviour, as we all do, but I always try to look beyond the offensive action and see if I can get into the mind of the perpetrator.

A person who is calm, has a healthy level of self-esteem, is loved and lives without needless fear is very unlikely to harm another being deliberately. It is those people in our society who have been hurt themselves who are more likely to be the perpetrators of gratuitous cruelty, whether physical or mental.

During the last few years a lot of publicity has been given to cases of child abuse and domestic violence. Time and time again it has been shown that people who abuse their children were once abused themselves. Battered wives are most often women who were physically abused by their fathers, and who see abuse as a form of love because no other manifestation of love was evident in their childhood.

People who have been hurt move on to hurt others. They seek to release their inner pain and anger by attacking another person, as though sharing the hurt within them will alleviate the deep insecurity and emotional pain that they suffer.

I recently read a powerful book called *An Evil Cradling* by Brian Keenan, an autobiographical account of the five years he spent in captivity in Beirut in the late eighties. For most of his imprisonment Keenan was incarcerated in a tiny cell and chained to the wall, and was made to suffer terrible abuse and cruelty.

The men who held him prisoner and were responsible for his day-to-day requirements were mainly young Moslem fanatics, products of a fierce and merciless regime and indoctrinated with the extreme ideology of Islamic Jihad. They were unloved and isolated within a violent world. They had never been educated or given the opportunity to feel or think for themselves, because they were always made to follow the orders of their militia leaders.

Keenan recognised the inner pain of these men even while he was himself suffering the outpouring of their hate and violence, and it helped him to keep his own identity in place. In other words, he realised that it was they who were truly the victims. It stopped him talking himself into the state of mind that I call 'victimhood', in which he would have begun to expect hurt and feel that he deserved it.

Keenan and his fellow prisoner John McCarthy were able with great bravery and fortitude to hold on to their sanity and strength. They would smile at these young men and refuse to bow down to them. I have no doubt that the key to their survival was their understanding of the gaolers, their acceptance of the fact that they were damaged souls to be pitied.

Keenan learned to accept and control the anger that welled inside him during the early assaults and used it to go deeper into his own psyche and innermost depths of his being. He used his captivity for his greater good and spent minimal time depleting his energy in the fruitless pursuit of hatred and thoughts of revenge.

There are many other cases where people have suffered dreadful cruelty and deprivation but have refused to give in to hatred, and have instead turned their experiences into opportunities for personal growth. Nelson Mandela is another great role model in this respect.

---

**Revenge is tomorrow's pain and suffering.**

---

## Avoiding the cycle of revenge

Hopefully, you will not have to face anything as dreadful as wrongful imprisonment, but we can all draw on the experiences of people like Brian Keenan in our everyday lives. When someone hurts you, think about where they are coming from. What is it that makes them aggressive? Look into their background and see if they themselves have been hurt and, if so, allow your compassion to come to the fore.

My stomach always curdles when I see footage of lynch

mobs and people baying for revenge after a murder. How will revenge bring back the precious life of the person who has been killed? All it does is perpetuate the cycle of misery. We see this in the Balkans, where the peoples are divided along lines of religion and nationality and locked into an endless and terrible cycle of attacks and reprisals.

As with all cases of violent or harmful behaviour, if the energy expended on revenge were used instead to heal both the victims and the perpetrators, then people would be able to move forward instead of becoming entangled in a vortex of retribution.

Forgiveness heals – it clears the way for inner peace.

## What forgiveness gives you

By trying to understand the motivation driving those who hurt you, you may be able to find a space in your heart to forgive them – but you may also wonder what good this will do you. The truth is that the opposite of forgiveness is hate and this emotion is harmful not only to the receiver but also to the giver.

If you have hatred inside you then you will feel the discomfort and disharmony it causes you emotionally, spiritually and eventually physically. It will burn inside you like a fire and destroy your peace of mind and any possibility of happiness. I am talking here about the inner happiness that each one of us ultimately needs and seeks.

By forgiving those who have harmed you, you can release the hate that holds you back to the past and to the person who hurt you. Hate will only stop you moving forward in life and back down the road of 'if only' and 'I should have'. Our happiness is to be found in the present not in the past. By mulling over the bad things that have happened to us we are sending our energy back in time and depleting our reserves for the present. We will become tired, depressed and unhappy, and unable to enjoy the good things that happen to us.

Holding on to the past stops people from creating fresh opportunities that bring with them new friends, jobs and rewarding experiences. Hatred is ugly and unfulfilling and the sooner you let it go the better for you on every count.

## Forgiving someone who has died

You may have an issue with someone who has died. This can be doubly hard to deal with because you may feel that it is impossible to do anything now – that it is too late. However, I shall shortly be introducing you to an exercise that will help you forgive and release, and which you can use not only in relation to the living but also to forgive those who are no longer here.

I have used this exercise myself with wonderful results. It gives you the opportunity to say things that you wished you had said or feel unable to say face to face. Remember the power of your thoughts: your intention to redress a situation will affect the soul of the other person or persons involved, whether they are still with you or have passed on.

Before I set out the forgiveness exercise, I would like to relate an experience I had when using it myself. I was actually right in the middle of the meditation when, all of sudden, the spirit of my father's father appeared in my mind's eye and asked forgiveness. I was taken aback, as I had forgotten all about the episode he must have been referring to.

My mother, father and myself had been staying with my grandparents for a holiday. One night I woke to hear raised voices and my grandfather shouting and swearing. I was shocked as my parents never argued and even now I don't recall them ever raising their voices apart from at this one time. Things got worse as the following morning we were literally thrown out by my grandfather, who was still incoherent with anger. I can still remember my grandmother weeping and my father's stern face as we left.

It was the last I ever saw of my grandfather as my mother and father never returned to his house again. I don't know or remember what caused the upset but it seemed my grandfather would often get abusive and physical after drinking spirits – it was not unusual for him to throw his dinner against the wall and shout at my grandmother.

Anyway, suddenly here was his spirit asking me to forgive him. I didn't find it difficult to do so since so many years had passed and the impact of the incident had faded in my mind. I therefore envisaged myself wrapping my arms around him and comforting him. Afterwards I was enthralled to see my grandmother appear and then my father. They both put their arms around him and all three of them went away together in peace.

So keep an open mind when you do this meditation and you may be surprised at who comes into your mind.

EXERCISE: TO FORGIVE

- Find a quiet place where you won't be disturbed.
- Close your eyes and breathe in deeply four times.
- See your roots grow down deep into the ground beneath you. Feel totally connected to the Earth.
- Now see yourself walking through a gate into a beautiful garden. Close the gate behind you and visualise this garden that is your private sanctuary. Take a few moments to be at peace and look around this beautiful place. See your favourite flowers and see the ponds and fountains which are set about in this serene and tranquil setting.
- Walk further and further into your garden until you come to an inner garden, a sanctuary surrounded by roses.
- Go right inside and feel the peace of this most private of places.
- See a bench in the centre of your rose garden, walk over and sit down.
- Call before you the person who you wish to forgive, asking them to join you.
- As they walk towards you, welcome them. Tell them why you were so upset with them and then forgive them.
- Put your arms around them and love them. Give them unconditional love – the love that holds no judgement, the love that accepts people for what they are.
- Ask yourself if there is anyone else who you need to forgive – keep your mind open to see who may come into the garden.
- Leave the garden in your own time and slowly come back into the room.

Well done. You should be pleased and happy with yourself because you have performed a very beautiful and loving act – bless you.

---

## Let Go Of Your Guilt and Forgive Yourself

Now we have looked at forgiving others, I would like to think about the great burden of guilt and the issue of self-forgiveness. Have you ever felt guilty? Do you carry this guilt with you now? Just take a moment to think about your life and see if there is anything you have done or said that you would like to retract – a part of your life where you would like to push the rewind button and replay with different words and different actions.

When I look back on something I regret, I find that the feeling of remorse comes and hits me in the stomach, often when I least expect it. It's like a deep wound that won't heal. It can be a particularly difficult burden to carry if the person who you feel guilty about has died or moved on out of your life.

There are many reasons why we may feel guilty. It could be that we have been hurtful or cruel to someone weaker than ourselves. We may have taken advantage of someone's generosity and open-heartedness. We may have been disloyal or unfaithful to a partner. We may have done something to ourselves that we regret. We may even now contemplate taking our own life when in a state of depression.

Whether you feel guilty about hurting yourself or other people, you need to forgive yourself. You would be amazed how much of our behaviour is as a result of an inner feeling of guilt. Even people who have been abused as children often grow up feeling guilty, as if they had in some way brought their suffering upon themselves.

Please, please don't continue to carry guilt. If you have hurt someone, do everything in your power to put the matter right, determine to avoid repeating whatever it was you did, then forgive yourself and move on. Sometimes just approaching the person involved and being totally honest can be a great help. They may well not feel as badly about whatever it is as you think, especially if it was a matter between family and friends.

Often getting the issue off your chest will relieve you of some of the guilt, and will stop the pain from turning into anger. It's incredible how we can sometimes manage to turn guilt around and become angry, not just with ourselves, but also with the person we have wronged, so putting severe strain on the relationship. I can't tell you exactly how to make retribution because each case will be different, but you will know what you have to do. If the person refuses to accept your apology then you still need to forgive yourself, let the issue go and get on with your life.

## Avoiding repetitions

Most people will forgive something once, but if you continue to hurt them in the same way then you are likely to lose the trust of the person involved. Once trust has gone from a relationship it is unlikely to survive. I can remember a time in my younger days when I sent a boyfriend packing just as he turned up to take me out. He looked at me surprised and asked why. 'You're twenty minutes late and you were late for every date before this!' I riposted. Even though he had always apologised for being late, he kept on doing it over and over again.

I saw his lateness as a lack of respect – you can take that attitude when you're young and attractive! I don't know if he learned his lesson. I have a habit of forgiving and forgiving and then suddenly reaching the end of my tether, whereupon I can't go back. Most of us have a limit to our patience!

---

**Learn the lesson, ask for forgiveness, forgive yourself and then move on, leaving the guilt behind you.**

---

Here is an exercise to help you.

---

EXERCISE: RELEASE YOUR GUILT AND BE FORGIVEN

- Find a quiet space where you won't be disturbed.
- Close your eyes and breathe in deeply four times.
- See your roots grow down deep into the ground beneath you. Feel totally connected to the Earth.
- See yourself entering a beautiful garden. Close the gate behind you and take a few moments to be at peace and look around this peaceful place. See the beautifully manicured lawns, the shrubs and trees which surround the garden. See your favourite flowers, see a pond with a fountain in its centre creating a spray of sparking diamonds in the sunlight.
- Enjoy the peace of your garden for a while.
- Walk further and further into your garden until you come to an inner space, a sanctuary surrounded by roses.
- Walk right inside the space and feel the peace and tranquillity of this most private of places.

- In the centre of your garden, see a bench, walk over and sit down.
- Call before you the person that you have hurt and ask them to join you. You may not see them clearly but don't worry, just acknowledge that they are present.
- Welcome the person. Tell them you wish to be forgiven. If you wish you may explain the reasons for your behaviour.
- Put your arms around them and love them. Ask them for unconditional love.
- Listen to them – they may have a message for you.
- When they have gone, look up and see a mirror image of yourself coming towards you – it is you.
- Walk up and take this reflection of you in your arms. Love and forgive as you would a child. Hold yourself close. Cherish and comfort yourself.
- Leave the garden in your own time and slowly come back into the room.
- Now let the matter rest – you have done all you possibly can. Let it go.

## Karma

Once we have forgiven others and ourselves we are ready to be in the state of love, in which we love others and ourselves unconditionally. Another great benefit of going through this powerful act of forgiveness is that we can clear our karma. I shall now endeavour to explain what I have learned about karma and what influence it has on our lives.

I was introduced to the powerful effect of karma in an amazing spiritual experience three years ago. I was sharing confidences with a girlfriend late one night in her kitchen. She was telling me the story of her mother and father's life together and her childhood experiences, especially the relationship she had had with her mother. It was a story filled with powerful and painful episodes of love and betrayal, kindness and cruelty, and I was totally enthralled yet appalled as she took me through the events that had brought her to where she is today. As she finished I said, 'My goodness that was karmic' – inferring that the forces of cause and effect had come through strongly in her words.

As I spoke a cold wind blew through the kitchen. I felt an enormous surge of energy start to flow around me. In my mind's eye I could see many events of the past involving her mother and father. In some images, one was abusing and hurting the other and in others the roles would be reversed, as I went through the many lifetimes they had spent together. It was like watching clips of a number of films and hearing sound bites.

All the while the energy, which was dark and cold, continued to flow past me. As I called for my guides and angels to help me take it away and clear this dark past, the electrical appliances in the kitchen were throbbing and pulsing and the fans were whirring. My friend was staring at me horrified, and I had to tell her to hold me in the light as the flow continued to wend its way past.

Eventually the energy flow stopped and the room returned to normal. I closed my eyes and meditated, asking for a reason for what had happened, although I strongly suspected that we had just seen the past and its dark emotions being cleared.

During the meditation a strong deep voice told me that I had been given the gift of clearing karma. I saw a brilliant white light while the voice continued to tell me of other gifts that would come in time. I felt my entire body fill with what seemed like high-speed energy, zooming through in a series of whooshes.

When I opened my eyes at last, my friend was again staring at me speechless, eyes round and mouth open. 'You, you, you,' she stuttered, 'you had a white light coming out of you.' We both sat back flabbergasted as we took in the inference of this disturbing event: I could clear karma. What a wonderful gift.

## What is karma?

Since then I have helped many people let go the great burdens of their past. Karma is the spiritual law that says what you give out you get back. So if you do a good deed, some blessing will surely come your way. Conversely, if you do someone harm then you will suffer accordingly.

In some countries the word is synonymous with fate – and so people resignedly accept all that comes their way in the belief that it is their karma so they can do nothing about it and are powerless to change their lives. I don't quite see it this way.

I see our karma as the natural result of our thoughts and behaviour. I see the pendulum that swings inevitably backwards after its forward thrust. The return swing can bring good or bad events, but these events are never meant as a punishment; rather they occur in order for us to learn. If you hit someone, for example, you can expect some retribution. It may not come from the victim of your aggressive act. We may feel terrible guilt, and this alone may be enough for us to learn that hitting someone is not beneficial in any way. Our behaviour will always bring about a return of some kind.

## Causes of karma

You may not always see what has caused the return swing of the pendulum. You may be going through a bad time in your life, for example, and not understand why. Many people have come to me saying they are blocked and cannot go forward in their lives, that everything seems to be against them. I always ask them first if they have tried being positive, knowing that, as we discussed earlier, our attitude and thoughts create much of our present karma.

I also ask them if they have any fears, as these are the most common obstacles in our forward path. If they have tried being positive and worked on their fears, and are convinced that there is nothing more they can do, I ask them if there is anyone they need to forgive. Then I take them though the process of forgiveness as set out in the meditation exercise I gave you earlier in the chapter.

Once they have genuinely forgiven all, including themselves, I know they are in a state where their karma can be cleared: the pendulum swing can be stopped. As I call for their karma to be cleared, I usually feel an enormous shift of energy as the dark and heavy energy of their past is lifted. The person normally feels much lighter as a result, as if they have had a heavy burden taken from them.

We have to feel the effect of our behaviour, but once we have accepted the message behind what has happened to us then we can let it go. By accepting the message, learning the lesson and forgiving others and ourselves we can clear our karma. It is easier to do this now, at this point in history, because we are receiving divine compensation and help. When Jesus came he cleansed us of our sins. He showed us that through love and forgiveness we

could be released from the sins of our past and step into
the 'kingdom of heaven', which I interpret as the state
of peace and inner happiness.

One of the hardest things about life is our seemingly
unreasonable and unjustified suffering and, though this
may be difficult to accept, we do sometimes make a
commitment before we are born to receive certain hardships or suffering. You may well wonder why we do this,
and it may be that we are seeking to further our personal
growth in a way that can only come through suffering.

If we wish to understand compassion, for example, we
need to know what it is like to suffer. In order to understand lack, we need to feel lack; in order to understand
the pain of others, we need to feel it ourselves. We grow
and develop through our challenges (I shall be discussing
the process of this evolvement in more detail in chapter
eight). Any suffering you are going through may therefore be as a result of a karmic contract, and only you can
let it go. You made this contract so you can break it. You
have complete free will and choice.

The following exercise will allow you to release your
karma.

EXERCISE: CLEAR YOUR KARMA
- Find a quiet space where you won't be disturbed.
- Close your eyes and say out loud, 'I release myself
  from all contracts and commitments that are now
  complete. I forgive myself and others completely. I
  release my karma now.'

In the past some ancient peoples would kill a sacrificial
lamb to achieve the same thing: they would put all their

fears and guilt into the lamb and give it to their gods in order to release karma – to cleanse their sins. Jesus is often referred to as the lamb of God – that is, the sacrificial lamb that died on the cross so that we could be released from our sins. I believe, and have seen for myself, that we can do this for ourselves. The key to successful cleansing is a total and absolute intent to forgive and be in the state of unconditional love in relation to every living being, including ourselves.

## Past Lives

As we now know, some of the events that we wish to clear from our lives may have occurred before this lifetime. I believe in reincarnation and I often see snippets of the past lives of my patients. Reincarnation is the continual process of birth, death and rebirth that we go through in our highest form. This highest form of our being is our soul. When we die our soul moves on in an etheric (energy) form and, after a period of time, returns to Earth through birth for another life. Although we don't have total recall of our past lives, they are an integral part of our make-up, of our highest form.

Our past-life experiences have contributed to our evolvement and it is through them that we become the person that we are today. This is why children of the same parents can have completely different personalities and characteristics. Each one of us is an amalgam of our genes, our upbringing, our current life experiences and our previous life experiences.

## How past-life experiences can affect us

Sometimes people are very obviously affected by their past-life experiences. They may have phobias, illness and fears that are rooted in this past. They may also have attractions to places, situations, food, etc., that they cannot explain or understand. These things are all distant memories that have come through to affect a person's current life.

If an event in a past life left an imprint upon our energetic body, we will carry the scar of this with us in this lifetime. The scar may result in a physical weakness: a death caused by a broken back in one lifetime may mean a weak back in this life, for example. Usually the only past-life experiences that come back to us or are imprinted on our energy body are those that involved highly charged emotions – say, for instance, the person's back was broken by a friend during an act of betrayal. Anyone who had been betrayed like this in a past life would probably also face issues of trust in this lifetime.

I have come across several people who have had issues of guilt to clear from their past. This guilt manifests itself as a lack of self-worth, and may be a factor in the number of people who suffer from eating disorders. In one such case I had, the young girl concerned had badly treated a partner in a past life who was also her partner in this one. She had a very turbulent relationship with him in this life, but she felt she owed him something and was therefore attached to him despite their troubles.

My patient had suffered from serious eating disorders since childhood but had never been able to understand what had triggered them. Her parents had always been loving and caring and there was nothing apparent in her early years that could have set off this problem. She did say that she had always felt a deep inner pain – similar to the feeling one gets with guilt.

I cleared her karma and encouraged her to forgive herself – not for her past actions, because she couldn't recall these herself, but for the abuse she had put her body through with her eating disorder. Last time I spoke to her she had definitely improved, and felt that any problem she now had was as a result of the habit that she had formed rather than any deep wound that needed healing. She had also resolved her relationship!

If you wish to go back into the past to look for the root cause of any problem, then I suggest you visit a good past-life therapist. A therapist will encourage you to see your past-life experiences by using a form of hypnosis that allows you to see and feel the situations that have caused your current problem. However, you may well be repeating the events or situations of your past life in this one, in which case you have the opportunity to heal the problem this time around. If you were not able to forgive someone who hurt you in a past existence, for example, you may be put in a position in this lifetime where you need to forgive someone for similar behaviour. So we have no absolute need to recall the past; we can still go through the process of learn, forgive and let go to clear the karma this time around.

## Living for the Moment

Before I leave the subject of karma and forgiveness, and to reconfirm my point that we need to let go our feelings of guilt wherever possible, I would like to bring your attention to one of the ceremonies performed by the Christian Church, the Catholic Church in particular.

To ensure that their members leave this Earth with a clear conscience and to give them ample opportunity to clear their consciences before leaving, Catholics are offered the 'last rites' at the point of their death. The last rites are all about us leaving this lifetime without guilt and, to me, the fact that they exist reinforces the essential teaching of forgiveness.

I personally feel that our lives would be happier if we considered every day to be our last, because we would then let go guilt and forgive others as we went rather than leave it to the last minute! It is essential that we strive to live for the moment and enjoy every minute we can. So do it now for you – release the past and enjoy the present.

You are nearly there. You are thinking positively. You have taken the best of your past and let go all that no longer serves you. You have forgiven yourself and others and moved into the state of unconditional love – you are well down your path of self-healing – fantastic – well done! I now want to introduce you to the concept of creating the life of your choice: of engaging your mind and letting your dreams come true. Carry on reading and I shall introduce you to the magic of the word *INTENT*.

# 7

# Developing the Power
of Your Mind

By calming and mastering our mind we can learn to focus
on the present, which is where we find happiness. Do you
worry about what might never happen? We look at ways
to handle stress. We see how Buddhists put themselves
into the state of peace by controlling their minds through
meditation. We discover how we can make real what we
need and want in life by using the power of our intent.

The mind is indeed a great source of power – or
perhaps I should say that it gives us access to a great
source of power. However, we can only make use of this
generator of power and energy if we have it within our
control. A mind that is unfocused and flighty is like riding
an unbroken horse: it will take you hither and yonder
without meaning or purpose. An undisciplined mind that
meanders from thought to thought can take over a
person's life, and lead them to vivid landscapes and
nightmarish situations that will disturb their peace and
cause untold stress.

It's my belief that stress is directly connected to an uncontrolled mind. Let's start by looking at the reasons why the mind becomes out of control, and then I shall show you how we can bring it into a state of peace. We can use this state of peace to draw in the things and situations that we desire.

## Stress

Stress is a modern-day phenomenon and a fashionable disorder. Everyone I know, whatever their lifestyle or job, seems to suffer from stress. They get stressed when shopping, driving or working. They get stressed with their partners, families and work colleagues. Stress is a state in which we are filled with anxiety – good old-fashioned fear again. Our muscles tense up, the adrenaline starts pumping and our heartbeat increases, all of which are symptoms of the state of fight or flight, our natural defence system.

This is an appropriate state to be in when we are faced with real, physical danger and our ability to fight back or run fast is essential for our survival, but it serves no purpose at all during a trip to the supermarket or when picking the children up from school – fighting and fleeing in these circumstances seems a bit drastic, doesn't it?

**Stress is a condition where the sufferer has a misaligned relationship with time.**

Stress is often caused by a time disorder – we get stressed because we fear that we won't have time to complete the agenda we have set ourselves. We may also get stressed when we take on jobs that are beyond us, ones for which we need more training or experience, because we fear failure. Stress, worry, concern – all these words are synonymous – and in nearly all instances they are caused by fear of something that may or may not happen in the future.

Worrying about the future and imagining the worst possible things that could happen is a dreadful waste of time and energy. Do you worry? Do you sit and fret? I know a number of people who are worriers and they cannot stop themselves; they know it is futile but it is like a compulsion or a habit that they cannot drop.

If you suffer unnecessary anxiety it may be that you don't know how to control your mind and that you are 'addicted' to worrying. As with all addictions, you will have to work hard to clear yourself of the problem.

You may also find that you have been influenced by your partner. Somehow worrying seems to be contagious and whereas you might once have been quite carefree and happy to take life as it comes, if your partner worries a lot, you may well start to worry yourself. I sincerely recommend that you endeavour to rid yourself of the worry habit, as it will prevent you from benefiting from a peaceful mind. However, since I realise none of us has a worry switch that can be turned off at will, I shall be showing you an exercise later in the chapter which will help you handle the problem.

## Focusing on the present

In order to combat any tendency you may have to worry about the future, I suggest we concentrate for a while on bringing ourselves into the present moment. This is where we find the true reality of our lives. It is in the here and now, not in the future and not in the past, that we shall find our peace. The past is over and done with and we can do nothing to change it.

In previous chapters we looked at ways in which we can release the gremlins of the old that come to haunt us, and let go the suppressed emotions that we carry with us as a result of past events. Now we shall look at living in this very moment – in current time or, as the technos call it, 'real' time.

Real-time living means enjoying the experiences that are taking place right now. To do this you need to rein in your mind to focus on what is going on around you. There are several exercises and processes that you can use, but I shall start with one that is simple and effective. It will bring in your scattered energy and also clear your aura of any negative energy blocks and thought forms. It will guide you into the present by making you focus on your breathing. It is excellent as a quick fix to calm yourself down and I suggest you do it several times a day – but first make sure no one is standing next to you!

---

EXERCISE: BRING YOURSELF INTO THE PRESENT
- Find a quiet space.
- Spread your arms out wide and then bring them into your body. As you do so, imagine you are pulling all your dispersed energy back into yourself.
- Repeat this process four times.
- Using your hands as combs, sweep around and down from your head.
- Repeat this sweeping action several times, until you feel calm and all the sticky energy around you has been released.

- Close your eyes, breathe in deeply four times and concentrate entirely on your breathing and nothing else. If you find this hard, try saying the words 'in' and 'out' to yourself as you breathe.
- Slowly come back into your surroundings. Repeat the exercise whenever you need to slow down.

---

An inability to focus on what is happening in the here and now encourages a butterfly mind that will take you off into the future and down the paths of the past. Although many people disparage it, I think the television can be a great help when people have a problem on their mind – it combines the benefit of bringing the viewer into the present while also giving them a break from their constant mind travel.

The programmes that I favour for their remedial powers are documentaries and comedies. Please avoid programmes that include violence if you suffer from any form of anxiety, as you will simply be allowing your subconscious to reconnect with traumatic experiences in your past, which may be the cause of your current problem. Reading, painting and other creative pursuits are also good for engaging the mind.

People suffer most from anxiety attacks at night because there are fewer distractions. In other words, at a time when we are not using our other senses to the fullest. The following process will encourage you to engage your powers of smell, sight, hearing, feeling and taste, and to disengage the mind.

---

EXERCISE: CONNECT WITH YOUR SENSES
You can do this exercise either sitting or lying down.
- Close your eyes and breathe in deeply four times.

- Now open your eyes and look around you. Focus carefully on everything you can see and closely observe their colour and form. Every time your mind goes off on a tangent, bring it back and concentrate on the colour of the thing you are looking at. Continue to do this for about five minutes.

- Look at all the objects you can see that are the same colour and notice how the colour varies slightly from object to object.

- Look at the shape and form of each object within your gaze, and see what shadows the object has created. Look at the grain in any wood that you can see; notice how the light reflects off any shiny or glass objects.

- Now close your eyes and listen. What can you hear? You will certainly be able to hear your own breathing – listen to the soothing rhythm of your breath. Now listen for a while longer. What else you can hear? Try harder and harder to hear and pick out the sounds around you. If your mind wanders, just pull your attention back and focus again on the sounds.

- With your eyes still closed, use your hands to touch all the things around you. Do this gently and slowly and in your mind see the pattern and image of what you are touching – concentrate on the smoothness, the roughness, ripples and ridges. Touch all your clothes if you are dressed. Touch your skin, feel your nails and your hands – does the feel of your skin change from the front to the back of your hands? Feel your hair, your face, eyebrows, lips, etc.

- Now move your attention to your mouth. What can you taste? Let your tongue move around your mouth, touching and tasting your teeth and your gums. Imagine different flavours and tastes that you enjoy.

Don't be surprised if your mouth starts to water as you engage your sense of taste.

- Now concentrate on your nose. Bring all your attention to your sense of smell. What can you smell right now? Each time you do this exercise, the more you will find to smell, but if you are having difficulty this time think instead of the smells that you love. Think of lavender and roses. Think of cinnamon and peaches.

You have now engaged all your real-time senses – well done.

---

## The Buddhist way

Buddhism is a belief system and a philosophy that involves the individual controlling his or her mind. Buddhists regard this mind control as the way to reach nirvana, or inner bliss. To help themselves achieve this they practise meditations in which they attempt to empty the mind completely.

I have introduced you to many guided visualisations in this book to help with your healing, but I would now like to look at this more purist form of meditation, which allows us to focus within ourselves and let go the busyness of our mind. There are several ways in which you can do this but I have selected two methods that I hope you will find reasonably easy and which can be practised at home, i.e. don't require you to go into retreat – even if the idea of a holiday in the Himalayas does appeal. (I have to confess I had the worst time during my 'retreat' in Tibet as I suffered from severe altitude sickness, so for me the hermit's cave is now out of the question!)

### Mantras

A mantra is a word or short sentence that you chant continually over a period of time. The effect is hypnotic and calming and pushes all other thoughts from the mind. Some mantras also call in the essence of a deity and can bring on amazing feelings of love and warmth once contact is made.

One of the mantras I enjoy is: Om Mane Padme Hum (pronounced, *'aum mahnay padmay hum'*). It is part of the Buddhist meditation 'Perimeta' and can help you purify and release the negative qualities it names:

| | |
|---|---|
| Om .................................. | Pride |
| Ma .................................. | Jealousy |
| Ni .................................. | Attachment |
| Me .................................. | Greed |
| Hum .............................. | Hatred |

Om Mane Padme Hum is associated with the Buddhist goddess of mercy, Kwan Yin, with whom I have a special relationship. I spent over six years living in the Far East, where many temples have been built in Kwan Yin's name, and my association with her became very strong during this time.

Kwan Yin looks over mothers and the sick, and many have felt her presence when using the mantra. Chanting Om Mane Padme Hum is not a form of worship and will not conflict with any of your other religious beliefs, as Kwan Yin is not committed to a religion. Just take your shoes off, sit comfortably and relax, holding your thumbs and first fingers together in what is called a 'mudra' (if you can sit cross-legged in the lotus position that's fine, but it's not essential). Repeat the mantra continuously for about fifteen minutes.

In the sixties, transcendental meditation (TM) became popular, especially when the Beatles took an interest and made a well-publicised trip to India. In TM you are given a personal mantra that is unique to you and, as with Om Mane Padme Hum, you say it continuously to induce peace of mind and wellbeing. There are still groups around the world that practise this method and you may find one near you. If you don't want to join a group then you can purchase a CD of mantras and accompany the recorded chants at home.

### Advanced meditation

Another meditation used by Buddhists to bring inner peace is one in which you visualise yourself as an inanimate object. A friend of mine did this recently – he spent half an hour as a pebble. At first he felt himself projected into a stream and then he settled gently on the bottom of the riverbed.

I was most impressed by his achievement as this method takes a great deal of concentration and demands complete mind control. If you want to give it a go, try it for just a few moments to start with and then gradually hold the focus for longer and longer. It is a process that has tremendous rewards and will certainly enable you to contain your anxieties once it is mastered.

## Isolation versus company

Having some space and time to be with myself is an essential part of my daily life, and I would hate to be always surrounded by others. A certain amount of solitude is balm for my soul. However, although there are many benefits to time alone and giving oneself space for contemplation, you shouldn't overdo it. Company can be great stimulation and can help take you out of depression or self-pity.

One of the best ways to be in the present moment is to be with other people, because when you are engaged in conversation and discussion you are totally present. I therefore don't recommend isolation and avoidance of company. Whatever your age, it is a good idea to meet up with others when and where you can, and to share your life rather than to shut yourself away. I realise these things are not always in our control and it can be hard to mix, especially if you suffer from depression or anxiety attacks, but having company will help.

My uncle is currently going through a terrible time. He is ninety-three, almost blind, recently lost his wife and has moved into a care home. He has lost all his comfort zones and now that his sight is going he has also become isolated. He feels as though he is in a virtual prison of semi-darkness. I feel so sorry for him. He is suffering all the symptoms of someone in solitary confinement – depression, nightmares, loss of focus and concentration, phobias and paranoia. However, although he lacks the stimulation of the full and interesting life that he used to lead, on the days that he makes contact with one of his old friends he feels much, much better and seems to rediscover some of his old self. I take it as proof that he is suffering mostly from a lack of interesting company rather than any actual sickness.

I know several much younger people who shut themselves away from the world because they find it too difficult to communicate and relate to others. If you know you are spending too much time alone, I ask you to do all that you can to mix, and find clubs and associations where you can meet other people with similar interests or even set up one of your own. The worst thing you can do is spend an excessive amount of your time away from other people as it will make it more difficult to heal any anxiety or worrying tendencies you may have.

## Mind Power

Once you have conquered your butterfly mind, or at least started to get your thoughts under control, you are in a position to access the power of this indefinable part of our being. I say 'indefinable' because there are few people who can truly say what the mind really is. It isn't your brain as this is the physical part of you that accesses your thoughts and memories and connects with your nervous system, glands and hence to your emotions.

I see the brain as a transmitting and receiving station – but it isn't your mind. My personal theory is that the mind is our local database: it holds a register of all the events and emotions that we have experienced. There is another, greater database that is generally inaccessible and which holds the memories of our other lives. Then there is an even greater database that holds all the thoughts and feelings of every living soul that ever existed. This larger database is commonly referred to as the Akashik records, and is the greater consciousness to which we are all connected. If our brains could receive messages from this source, then we could tap into the minds of all. Psychics and clairvoyants have the ability to make this link so it's not an impossibility.

I believe that if we did manage to connect with the greater consciousness, then we would be using the full extent of our brains. The medical profession says that much of our brain is redundant on a daily basis and some of it is never used. I think we use more of it at night when we dream, and that in the not too distant future we will be able to perform acts and see and understand things that at the moment are beyond our realisation.

When we have learned how to harness the full powers of our brain, we will all be telepathic and able to extend our use of our sixth sense, which allows us to know and understand things that are not seen or obvious to the naked eye.

I also believe that when a person's brain is damaged, it is the receiving station that is damaged not the actual memory or database of past events, and that therefore, if we could train another part of the brain to do the same job, we would be able to retrieve the memory. In fact, I don't believe our mind, our memory or even our thoughts are actually in our head at all – I believe they are held in the etheric bodies around us, in the great databases in the sky! But wherever you believe the mind is, once we have settled it down and stopped it jigging about constantly there is no doubt that we can start to use it in the most amazing way.

## Manifesting

How would you like to control the weather on important days, or bring in the money you need to meet your bills, or find your dream home or the job that will truly fulfil you? You can, you really can. It's called 'manifesting' and it enables you to bring about your desires, providing they are for your highest good. I say 'for your highest good' because there are things that we desire from time to time that wouldn't bring us happiness. Huge amounts of money, for example, don't necessarily bring happiness, as is shown by the lives of some lottery winners and heirs of great fortunes. In fact, money rarely brings happiness when it hasn't been earned by our own endeavours.

Manifesting is a simple process and it will help you achieve and receive all that you need and want. I use it to bring into my life not only the things I need for my work, but also to draw the people in that I need to help me solve problems and to assist me achieve my dreams.

This magical process requires a couple of vital ingredients – but don't worry, they don't include any part of a toad and I won't be asking you to go to the crossroads at midnight! No, the two essential ingredients are: *consistent intent* and *faith that it will happen*. I would also add a dose of patience, as divine timing is often involved and this means that you cannot always be particular about when the manifestation will take place. Just be patient and stick to your convictions. I cannot explain exactly how this process works but I know that it does. It is another aspect of the law of cause and effect and it is extremely powerful.

Let's look at consistent intent first. You have to have a reasonably stable mind before you can perform these feats because you will need to keep your aim, dream, need or requirement clearly and consistently in your mind. It doesn't have to be there all the time; in fact, once I have put out the requirement I tend to let it go completely. But you can't keep changing your mind about what it is you want or you will be sending out mixed messages – meaning the energy pattern of your wish will get muddled and your manifestations will not work.

You will also need faith that the process will work, and once you have expressed your need, stop fretting and worrying about the result. Any worry diminishes the chances of a successful outcome because, again, it muddies the waters of your mind. Once you have made your announcement, leave it to the universe and God to give you what you want and in the way that will suit you best. We always get our wishes fulfilled but not necessarily in the way that we expect them. For example, you may need some money and hope for a pay increase at work but instead get a windfall from the tax office (unlikely as that may seem!). Or you may be offered a job that not only suits you better than your current one but pays more as well. Just writing about it reminds me of what a wonderful, exciting process it is! – I urge you to try it out as soon as possible.

There are several things to remember when manifesting:

- Use it only for the greatest good of all. Never try to use it for the detriment of another person, or the law of cause and effect will treat you badly.
- Do it with love and do it with sincerity.
- Always request that what happens will be for your greatest good. We can't always see the bigger picture of our lives and so don't always know what would be best for us in the long term.

So now you are ready, here we go . . .

---

EXERCISE: MAKE YOUR DREAMS COME TRUE
**Step 1**
Decide what it is you really want, whether this is wealth, happiness, success at work, a partner, a new job, a sunny day for your wedding, a taxi, a parking space, or whatever. Be absolutely sure that you are clear about what you want and think hard about whether it would bring you happiness.

**Step 2**

*Intend* that you will have your wish: know it and feel the knowing go deep inside you with no doubts whatsoever – after all, you deserve it. Make contact with your heart chakra in the middle of your chest and feel your intention coming from this energy centre. Your heart chakra oversees all matters pertaining to love in your life and the flow of loving energy. Say the words of your wish out loud – for example, 'I would like to receive enough money to pay off my mortgage, providing this is for my highest good.'

**Step 3**

Envisage yourself receiving your wish: close your eyes and see it happening clearly and strongly. If you have difficulty visualising it, then just sense it coming to you.

**Step 4**

Let go. Pass the ways and means of the manifestation you have wished for over to God – safe in the knowledge that whatever will occur will be for your highest good. At this point you need faith. Remember that very often we get our wishes granted but not as we expect them. Remember also that what may seem like setbacks are often blessings in disguise.

---

I have a dear group of friends who are the core members of the Hearts and Hands organisation in Malaysia. One of them is a healer and she gives much of her life to healing the sick and poor from all around the country. In return for her services she simply asks for a donation, and she and her husband (who gave up his job to drive her around) survive on whatever money she is given. As a result, they never have much to spare.

My friend has a clinic that she runs from her home, and a while ago she decided that the house needed a make-over. Apart from getting it redecorated, she also wanted to add a small extension so that she could give her patients a washroom. She called in the local builder and he gave her a quotation of 13,000 Malaysian ringgit, which is a fair amount of money. Since she had no means of getting hold of that kind of sum, she decided to manifest it.

She sat down and followed the process I have described and, with her heart wide open, let her intent pour out to the universe. She asked God to fulfil her need, providing it was for the highest good and the benefit of all.

To help the process along she decided to buy herself a lottery ticket. There is a lottery in Malaysia where you can put your car number into a weekly draw. So my friend sent off her application and sat back to see what would transpire.

In the draw for the first week she was unlucky, but in the second week's draw – which also happened to coincide with her birthday – she won. You may ask how much she won but, of course, it was 13,000 ringgit! Needless to say, she was a very happy lady and I have to admit her experience shored up the belief systems of all who know her!

When you are deciding what it is that you truly want be sure to use your feelings rather than your head. You may want to use a pendulum or use the kinesiology test (as discussed in chapter two) to check that you are wishing for what you truly want. Another way to check out your plans is to discuss them with someone else – not so as to get their opinion but to see how strongly you put your case across. I often talk to a friend about plans that I have and see how they sound when I spell it all out. Sometimes my ideas come across as weak and watery and then I know that they aren't really for me.

### SYMBOL FOR MANIFESTING – THE WISH SYMBOL

This symbol tells the universe that you are making a wish. It is very powerful so take care when you use it! Whatever you are holding in your mind will be manifested.

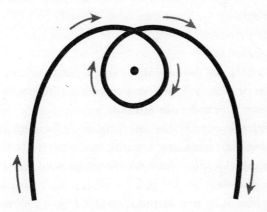

*Start drawing from the bottom left and finish with the dot. While you do this, say, 'I manifest . . . (whatever you wish for), if it is for my highest good.'*

### *Help yourself*

Of course, it's no good putting out your intent to receive or change something in your life if you don't put in some effort as well. It's that old maxim 'God helps those who help themselves.' Your efforts should be consistent with your needs. The process isn't going to work if you wish for lots of money and then refuse to take a job, for example, or wish for a loving partner and then stay with someone who abuses you. You and you alone are responsible for your life.

## The time line

Another way in which you can influence a future event is by using the time line exercise. It's quite simple and it's great for bringing sunshine or ensuring that important events go smoothly. I use it all the time and it never fails me. The essential ingredients are, once again, intent and belief.

---

EXERCISE: USE THE TIME LINE TO BRING SUCCESS
Use this meditation to enhance any future event, either for yourself or for your friends.
- Find a quiet place where you won't be disturbed.
- Close your eyes and breathe in deeply four times.
- Visualise a line which has dates marked along it.
- See the date of the event that you wish to affect.
- See the line at that point covered in sunshine and a great shower of golden sparks; see rainbows and any other aspect of a happy event that come to mind.
- If it's an event where you wish for success, see champagne corks flying and people raising their glasses.
- See the Sun shining and blue skies.
- See many happy smiling faces and everyone having fun.
- Now open your eyes and let the universe do its work.

---

I shall end this chapter with a true story that shows the power of the mind. Please use the technique for yourself soon – you will be amazed at the results.

This, believe it or not, is a true story and verifies all I have been telling you about manifesting with intent. It was one of my earliest experiences of the power of this process.

A few years ago I held a workshop at my home in the New Forest in Hampshire, England. Four of the people attending worked together. I knew two of them personally, and they were my house guests. The other two – let's call them Pete and Jo – were staying in the local guesthouse in the village and had brought their wives with them to make it a short holiday (while they attended the workshop, their wives planned to go sightseeing).

At some point during the second day of the workshop I began explaining to the attendees that once they started to heal and became open to their intuition, they would start to find synchronicity creeping into their lives. Synchronicity is the term used to describe apparent coincidences, which are actually the result of the attraction of like energy. To give them some examples, I said that they may find that they get given the same book by two different people, or that the same suggestions and ideas come up in different conversations, and so on.

Suddenly Jo got very excited and started stabbing his notes with his finger. 'Look at this!' he cried. He had his finger on the paragraph on positivism and keeping an upbeat attitude to life. I had written that singing is a particularly good way to lift the spirits and suggested the song 'Always Look on the Bright

Side of Life'. 'I don't believe it!' he shouted. 'I was
only singing that this morning.' Jo was truly excited.
'Would you believe it?' he said again. 'My wife virtually threw me out of the room because I was getting
on her nerves so much – me being so cheerful so early
in the morning.'

We were all flabbergasted; even I felt that this was
an amazing confirmation of my point. The song in
question is from the film *The Life of Brian* and was
popular years ago, but it isn't one that you hear played
much any more. Yet Jo had sung it on the same day
that I had planned for us to discuss it. It was
synchronicity working already for sure! For the rest of
our time together Jo and Pete would go off each
evening singing the song and it became the workshop's
theme tune.

The following week my friend rang me to tell me
that it was Pete's birthday and asked me if I wanted
to join them as they were all going to get together at
the pub near their office in London. Apart from the
fact that London is a two-hour car journey from my
house, I had plans to visit a relative for the day. I
declined but said, 'Tell Pete I will be there in some
way and that I will be giving him a sign.'

When I had hung up, I closed my eyes and, using
the time line method, put myself in the pub. I thought
they might be a little late so added half an hour to the
time they had given me. I put out the intent that there
would be a sign – I didn't say what it should be,
although I thought it would be great if it could be our
workshop song. It even crossed my mind to ring the
pub and ask them to play it, but I didn't know the
name of the pub or the address so it was too difficult.
In the end, I left it to the universe.

On my return that evening I had a call from Pete. 'Thanks for my present,' he said, 'but how on earth did you do it?' He went on to tell me what had happened at the pub. They had turned up late (as I had predicted) and found the place full except for one table with six seats, unreserved but empty. Pete had smiled and said, 'It's Anne's present.' Then they bought their drinks, sat down, and were raising their glasses to toast the birthday and their present, when over the pub's piped music system came 'Always Look on the Bright Side of Life'. When Pete ran up to the bar to ask who had selected it, the barman said, 'Oh no, sir, we can't select the songs. It's all done by random selection.' Talk about synchronicity!

# 8

# The Soul – Healing
# and Connecting

What is our soul? What happens to our soul when we die? How can we pull ourselves together to heal a fragmented soul? In this final chapter, we make the soul connection and let our intuition flow. What is our life's purpose and what help can we expect? We discover the power of distance healing.

The soul is the most precious part of our being. It is the highest form of our self. It is the part of us that represents our greatest achievements and is our most evolved aspect. It is the divine – the spark of God within. If we can connect with our soul, we can connect to the entirety of life.

## God: the Source of all Life

We are all created from the consciousness that is God, or the Great Spirit, or Yahweh, or All That Is, or whatever your name is for the divine presence that is the source of all life. If you don't mind, I shall be conventional and refer to God.

Although I feel comfortable with the name God, I should say that this is not God as represented in the Old Testament and various other ancient manuscripts; this is not a God of retribution and wrath, a domineering and overpowering presence that demands instant obedience. Of course, in the days that these texts were written it was by showing exactly these qualities that society's rulers held their people in submission, and so it is not surprising that they portrayed their divine leader in the same way.

As mankind has generally evolved and we have come to expect more compassion and care from our leaders, our perceptions of God have also changed. Nowadays we see God as a loving and benevolent presence. Jesus came and told us that God was not the ogre as had been previously portrayed in the days of Abraham, and now we have moved forward once again to realise that God is accessible to all.

I call this new direct form of spiritual activity and belief 'personal spirituality'. We do not need to worship God through institutions or other people. We can make our own personal connection and communication with the divine.

As humankind continues to evolve, so will our understanding and perception of God. Whereas God was once seen exclusively as a male presence, for example, the female aspects of the divine are now acknowledged and respected, as we acknowledge and respect the power of the female in our society. To appreciate God in a modern light, read the books of Neale Donald Walsch. In his wonderful series *Conversations with God*, Walsch relates his own personal experiences of communicating with the divine and in so doing introduces a God that is of our age.

---

God created everything. Therefore God is everything.

---

## Feeling and sensing the presence of God

I am often asked how I know that God exists. My answer has to be that you can only truly believe if you have felt or sensed the power and presence of a divine presence at some time in your life. These connections vary from person to person but I have experienced a variety of such sensations, many of which I know have been felt by lots of other people.

You could start by being open to the notion that anything that cannot be explained or seen with the naked eye but that gives you a tremendous feeling of joy is the work of a higher force. My personal experiences of God have come from first, my opening my mind to the possibility of his existence and second, the fact that on several occasions I have been overcome with a huge rush of energy that has filled me with such love and joy that it has brought tears to my eyes. Only some of these experiences have been awe-inspiring but all have left me with the unmistakable knowledge of having been in the presence of something quite wonderful. I have had these feelings when watching a sunset, walking through woods, sitting by the sea near my house in France, and also in my kitchen, while staying at a guesthouse and on an aeroplane!

Many other people see and sense God in nature, in great music and in fine art. We all have our own sense of the divine, as understood through different experiences and on various occasions. I would like to tell you about my most powerful connection with God, which happened while I was travelling between Singapore and Kuala Lumpur in Malaysia.

While on a visit to Singapore, where I was giving some workshops and healing sessions, I had a psychic reading from a dear friend of mine. My friend told me that I was about to open my heart chakra and that the experience would increase my healing abilities. You will recall that the heart chakra is where we receive and give love, and as love is the essential ingredient for healing others, I could see how my heart being completely open and clear would be most beneficial for my work.

My friend then went on to tell me that in order for this to happen I would have to forgive God. I couldn't understand this at all – it seemed an astonishing thing to say! – so I asked her to explain. She told me that in one of my past lives, in South America, I had seen my people (I was a spiritual leader at that time) being massacred by conquistadors. Since then, she said, I had become detached from God and held feelings of anger for him in my heart.

I meditated on my friend's message and as I did so, I saw a huge troop of soldiers marching into a valley. My most significant and overwhelming memory was that they were carrying a cross. During this regression I could feel the emotions of anger and hate rising in me again as I connected the destruction of my culture and people with the symbol of Christians and their God. I was killed shortly afterwards in this past life so my feelings of anger had been imprinted upon me, and had stayed with me even until this, my current lifetime.

To help me get over my emotional block – this anger
I felt towards God for letting this past event happen
– I performed the forgiveness exercise (*see page 188*).
I felt a great deal of relief as a result. Although I had
always believed in God and had felt his love on many
occasions, I had often had a problem talking about him
in my workshops. And when I had talked to him I had
always felt his response as if from a long way away,
above my head.

Two days after this I left Singapore on the early
morning flight for Kuala Lumpur. I was surrounded
by businessmen, most of whom were busy reading the
morning papers and preparing themselves for their
day's meetings. I had my breakfast and then, just as
we were beginning our descent to K.L. airport, I closed
my eyes and started to meditate.

I felt myself offering my heart up to the great light
I could see above me. It was a spontaneous giving of
my heart to God. This in itself was wonderful, but
then an amazing thing happened – I saw a pair of
beautiful hands that were filled with light returning
my heart, which had been transformed into gold. I
sensed this 'new' heart entering my heart centre and
I was filled with the most amazing feelings of love
and happiness. I promptly burst into tears just as we
landed – much to the concern of my fellow passen-
gers! I left the plane on an incredible high and with
a huge grin on my face, surrounded by intrigued businessmen (who must have thought I was completely
dotty!).

I can now hear God speaking to me much closer to
home, in my heart. And I also found that my healing
powers increased, as my friend had told me they would,
but only when my heart had finally opened completely

through another experience of God, which I had later that year in Tibet.

---

Look for the divine presence in the mundane – in the everyday events of our life. Every act of kindness, everything that has beauty, everything that helps us in any way – that is God.

---

Please excuse me for referring to God as 'he' throughout this text. There are, of course, two aspects of God and the female Goddess is particularly prevalent and powerful at this time. You can use any name you like, whether it be God or Goddess, creator, source, spirit, or any name that sits well with you. My only wish is that you have or will have an experience of divine presence at some time in your life.

At the end of this chapter I shall be sharing an exercise with you that I use when I want to connect to my soul presence, and from there step into the light which represents the presence of God. I hope you will also find that it helps you make that special connection.

## Our Soul

I believe that our soul is that part of us that is closest to God, in as much as it is the highest form of our being. If we accept that God created us and he is all that is, and that our soul is the permanent and ongoing part of us, then our soul must be a part of God.

We are now tasked with the question of where the soul is. Some Indian faiths believe it is situated behind the third eye in our brow, which is why some Indian women wear a protective dot there. Some believe it resides in our solar plexus. I don't truly know, but I suspect it is in every part of us, in a similar way that our energy body runs through and around us. However, for ease of visualisation, I like to project my soul symbolically about a metre above my head.

As it is the least dense form of ourselves, the soul cannot be seen by mortal eyesight, but a psychic will be able to see it, and the causal body that sits around it. I used to know a great healer and psychic who was able to squint and see all of this quite clearly. He was able to read my potential by seeing what I had achieved in the past and what knowledge and wisdom I had the ability to access in this lifetime.

The causal body that sits around the soul is like a personal library where everything we have ever learned is stored. Unfortunately, we don't get to access all of it – only what we need as we evolve through this life cycle – but it affects our personality and character. Hence those people who we consider to be 'old souls', who have a depth of wisdom and knowing about them which is not easily definable but which we can sense.

An old soul has been on its journey for some considerable time; it has repeated the cycle of life and death many times and has evolved beyond any need to carry hatred and the darker emotions. Old souls come into life with an innate wisdom and seem to have a sense of knowing even as children. You must have come across a child who seems to look at you with the eyes of a sage.

Souls are created by God from himself. This means that the same life force flows through all of creation, from flowers to humans. Some thinkers maintain that human souls are created from the souls of animals. It is also believed that most animals have group souls rather than individual ones but that when we domesticate them, as we do when they become our pets, they develop their own personality, character and soul definition. These domesticated animals might then come back in human form in one of their future reincarnations. Personally, I think my dogs are too good to come back as humans – they can certainly teach us a thing or two about unconditional love!

## Soul and spirit

I should explain the difference between the spirit and the soul as I see it, although in many instances the words are used synonymously. I believe that our spirit is like the aura of our soul. It is our connection to the spirit of all, which is God. Souls that have lost their way (lost souls) are souls that have lost this vital connection, that is, they have lost their spirit. Hence people who are in this state have no light in their lives whatsoever. They wander through life with no means of connecting to the greater consciousness, the rest of life.

## The beginning of the cycle of life

It's difficult to know where to begin when describing a cycle, but I may as well start with the connection that the soul makes once it has chosen its new parents. That's right, we choose our parents. Our choice is determined partly by the sort of life experience we wish to have this time around and partly by the soul connections we have made in previous lives. We prefer to reincarnate with groups of souls that we already know, and we connect with different groups throughout our lives depending on what we are going through at any particular time. I have a family soul group, for example, and several soul groups in different parts of the world who are involved in healing and teaching.

Once we have decided on our prospective parents we await conception. This is the point at which the soul first makes contact with its physical body. It then moves in and out of the foetus as it is forming within the womb. I have read many conflicting reports regarding at what point exactly the soul becomes attached to the human form. My personal interpretation is based on the experiences I have had when working with expectant mothers and from talking to a friend who was present when his wife gave birth.

## A baby's soul

When I lived in Malaysia I held a regular Monday morning gathering for anyone who needed healing. Some friends of mine who had also learned to heal would get together to help each other and anyone else who felt we could assist them in some way. One of our group became pregnant and throughout her pregnancy she would come for a weekly 'zap', as we called our healing session. She found it both calmed her and gave her great comfort.

I have always believed that the baby feels all its mother's emotions and therefore is affected by whatever the mother experiences, both good and bad. I hear this has now been confirmed by the medical profession, which recently announced that anxious mothers have anxious babies. It seems to me completely obvious that this should be so, as mother and baby are so completely attached. It is therefore important that an expectant mother be as relaxed as possible. But please don't start feeling guilty if you had a difficult time when expecting – remember that everything has a reason and both you and your baby will have needed that experience in some way.

While we were healing our pregnant friend one Monday morning, I suddenly became aware of a light presence in the room. It was a bright little ball of energy and it flew around the room like a butterfly, and was then absorbed into my friend. My friend felt a feeling similar to gentle butterflies in her stomach at the same time.

I realised, of course, that this was the soul of her baby. However, I believe that this was only a 'hello' visit and that these can happen on many occasions before the actual birth. (My friend was about five months pregnant when it first happened.) In my view, the soul only takes up permanent residence at the actual time of birth – when the baby comes fully into the world.

## What happens when we die?

So the soul is in residence from birth, and will stay there in most cases until the physical form that we have taken for this lifetime is either worn out or we have moved on. Eventually, once it recognises that we have extracted all that we need from this life, our soul makes a plan to exit. This can be an 'accident' or an illness.

Shakespeare had incredible perceptiveness, and his analogy of life being a stage feels very good to me. We are all players who pick up our costume – our human body form – then make our entrance – our birth – then act out our part to the best of our ability – that is, live our life – before making a final bow and leaving the stage – our death, at which point we step back into the real world.

> We are energy and energy can never be destroyed –
> it can change its form but it can never be destroyed.
> Death is a transition from one state of energy to
> another.

If death is merely a transition from one way of life to
another it is nothing to fear. Of course, we are bound to
experience some trepidation when stepping into the
unknown, but you have probably noticed that when
people are close to death their resistance decreases. Very
often, a peace will come over people as their knowledge
of the inevitable comes to them.

When we die, our soul leaves our body and moves
through a tunnel to a great light that indicates the higher
realms of existence. We are met by family members and
friends, and also by any spiritual leader or teacher who
we would expect to be there. Our ability to manifest is
paramount in our new home and we create the world
around us that we expect and desire. This is heaven. If
we are filled with guilt and expect a bad time when we
die, we create a hell that we will suffer until we can learn
to move through it.

There are several good books about the death experience and the afterlife. One that I think is very comforting
for people who have recently lost a loved one is *Embraced
by the Light* by Betty Eadie. Her knowledge of the astral
plane, which is where we go when we die, is based on a
near-death experience that she had a few years ago. Eadie
describes libraries where we can increase our knowledge
of life and find teachers who can guide us. For those who
arrive traumatised by their death or who were seriously
ill before they arrived, there are nurses and counsellors

to help with their transition. My original guide, my grandmother, is now one of these beings, helping souls on their arrival.

One of the first things we do when we arrive in heaven is go through a life review. We look at everything we did and examine how we reacted to our challenges – rather like watching an autobiographical video. We are not punished for what we have done (there are no avenging angels waiting to lay into us for our crimes!). However, we are encouraged to review our actions and see where we could have done better. We then spend some time determining what we need to learn and taking advantage of the help that surrounds us. After a period of time we may decide to return to Earth for another life.

Earth is an excellent school. While we are here we have free will to make our own choices. The fact that we forget all that went before means we start with a clean slate, aside from the innate wisdom and knowing that we carry in our soul, and which comes through in our character and personality.

If we decide to return to Earth, we then choose an appropriate date for our birth – the position of the planets will have a bearing on our personality and the events that will be drawn to us in our life. Since we are also the product of our genes we also have to choose the parents that will give us what we need. Finally, we make plans with our soul groups to decide on the work we will do together.

---

We arrive, we grow, we learn, we leave, we arrive, we grow, we learn, we leave . . .

---

## Here we go again! What is your purpose?

Once the time and date have been set for our birth then we get ourselves prepared for our new existence. We may have worked hard to rid ourselves of any residual emotional trauma from our last life but some fears will probably come with us on our return journey. We will also bring hidden loves and preferences for food, countries, music and other aspects of this world's many offerings, and these will be apparent even in our early years. So the cycle begins again.

Eventually, once we are truly enlightened, we will no longer need to come to Earth to grow; our further evolution will take place on other, higher levels of existence. We may, however, come back to Earth to help others. There are many such souls on Earth right now since humanity requires many helping hands to meet some of its current challenges. We seem to be hell-bent on destroying our school! These helpful souls are often referred to as 'light workers' and many of you reading this book will have agreed to play some part in this aid scheme.

## Bringing in light

The purpose of your life may involve bringing light and love to Earth and spreading it to all you meet. It is unfortunate that most people live only for themselves; if we all spent just a short time each day considering others we could make a huge difference.

Every time you smile at someone instead of criticising them, every time you show patience in frustrating situations and every time you forgive someone for even the smallest misdemeanour you are bringing light into the world. The very act of self-healing and working through your own issues will be helping the world because we are all connected through the life force energy and, therefore, as each one of us raises our vibrations we affect the rest of humankind and the planet.

At the end of this chapter I shall be showing you how you can actively make a difference through distance healing. You may have been given a bigger role: to teach and encourage people to move to a state of love and help them to find inner peace in these turbulent times. Whatever your role, it is important and will have a noticeable effect on the evolution of the planet and all who live upon her.

## We may face difficulties

Some souls are not totally prepared for their return journey or may have given themselves too hard a task to fulfil in this lifetime. They may have bitten off more than they can chew. This means their time here will be a struggle – they may even find they cannot cope and eventually take their own life.

I am glad to say that society doesn't regard suicide as the disgrace it once did. It wasn't so long ago that the Christian Church wouldn't allow a suicide victim to be buried in consecrated ground, as it was considered a crime against God to take your own life. That said, it is a cause of great sadness when a young person becomes so distressed that they give up on their life, and they deserve all our love and compassion.

Occasionally, a life purpose can be achieved quickly, and we may only need a few weeks or months of life. In these cases of infant mortality it is the parents who suffer the most and therefore we have to trust that this was also their karma, their wish for greater learning that brought this situation into their life.

In other circumstances we may have made a commitment before we were born to help a soulmate by leaving
them early, so that they can learn from the experience,
as is the case when a mother dies young and leaves her
children.

I should stress that there is no stigma attached to the
suffering that any soul experiences – it is not a matter of
people deserving the problems they encounter or even
creating them on a conscious level. This kind of thinking
can bring on guilt and that is certainly not the purpose.
The idea is rather to realise that everything that happens
to us is for a reason. We must make the most of whatever happens and learn, rather than spend the rest of our
lives being torn apart by our earlier experiences.

## Soul Connection

Although we are not aware of our previous lives when
we are born and not always aware of our purpose on
Earth, we learn more of this as we progress through our
lives. As I have said, our soul is our highest level of
knowledge and understanding and the more closely
connected we can be to it in our lives, the more we can
organise and create a life that is in tune with our highest
needs. If we are connected to our soul we are in touch
with our intuition, which is the way our soul relates to
our consciousness, our everyday thinking and feeling.

Some people seem to be totally in touch – they work
with their intuition or 'gut feeling' all their lives. There
are many paths that we can take on our journey, all of
which will get us to where we need to be, but some paths
are harder and rockier than others. The path you walk
depends on you. As you make each decision at each cross-

roads you determine your path. The more in touch you are with your inner self, your inner feelings, the easier it will be for you to choose a route that will be smooth and less traumatic.

Let's think about how this works on an everyday level. We make many decisions that affect the direction of our lives: we choose partners, homes, jobs, etc. All these are major decisions and if we base them on logic rather than intuition and feelings, we are likely to take ourselves down a difficult route. Although no choices can be said to be actually wrong, some will result in us facing greater challenges.

In my early thirties I had a strong desire to be a saleswoman. I was working as a training manager for a computer company at the time, which had operations throughout the world. I wanted more of a challenge and so I asked if I could join the sales team. The then sales director was against the idea of having women in the sales force, but the more he tried to dissuade me the stronger I pushed for the position. He proposed instead that I take a training role with more responsibility and although it sounded quite attractive, with plenty of challenges and opportunities for travel, my pride and ambition drove me to push for the sales job.

If I am honest, I can acknowledge that there was a little doubt inside of me, like a small worm wriggling, telling me that sales wasn't really for me. However, determination won the day and I was finally given what I wanted: I spent the next four years travelling the world selling computers.

I spent time in Greece and Turkey, South Africa and Nigeria, India and Pakistan. It was a hard row. I was alone most of the time in cultures that were at best unsupportive of women, and at worst outright chauvinistic and antagonistic. I faced hardships and challenges that I suppose gave me an inner strength, but it wasn't easy.

Looking back I can see that I learned a lot and I have benefited from the traumas that I experienced. I am aware that no experience is wasted and that all that happens is meant to be. But I could probably have acquired the same knowledge by doing the other job and also had a much easier and fun time. So, Jerry, you were right! I made my choice based on pride and ambition rather than listening to my inner voice, my intuition.

Now I am in touch with my soul and I make my choices totally according to my gut feeling. My life is much easier as a result. You are probably wondering how we can make this soul connection. It is actually a process that we work on throughout our life, and it can take anything from two minutes to a lifetime. I have been leading you through the process in this book: you began by taking a positive attitude and view of all that happens in your life; you then let go your fears and old emotional blocks and stepped into the state of love; you cut the cords of past relationships and improved on your current ones; finally you cleared your karma with forgiveness. In summary, there are four main steps:

1. Becoming positive.
2. Moving from fear to love.
3. Forgiving all.
4. Connecting with your soul.

When we have looked at the situations that can harm our relationship with our soul, I shall show you an exercise to help heal it and make the connection.

## Lost or damaged souls

When someone experiences a particularly frightening or traumatic event they can become detached from part of their soul. In some cases of abuse, for example, a child will leave the aspect of themselves that suffered behind, as they seek to shut out the memory of what happened. This is a useful survival instinct, but at some time during this person's evolution they will need to recapture and heal the part of them that they cut off and left behind.

My first encounter with a fragmented soul was when I was healing a young man who had difficulty enjoying life. He told me he could never fully give himself to a woman and also felt unable to commit to his work totally. As a consequence, he felt he was only half living his life. People who experience this type of half-life can often become out of touch with their capacity to love and this makes it difficult for them to have deep and fulfilling relationships.

I was healing the young man in my normal way when I felt a great pain in my back and I sat down beside him. I then heard my guide speaking to me (we shall look at spirit guides and the role that they play a little later in the chapter). My guide instructed me to stop my usual healing process and to sit quietly. He then led me on a journey that took me back into the life of my patient. I was shown some of the young man's earlier life experiences and witnessed some of the traumas that had affected him.

At one point I saw a small boy crying and hiding under a bed. I called to the boy, encouraging him to come out, and when he did, I gave him a huge hug and lots of love. Gradually the boy stopped crying and I picked him up and carried him with me for the rest of the journey. I healed the young man each time I saw him in distress as a young boy, and then I brought that aspect of him back and placed it in his heart centre. I sat for a while afterwards and envisaged the man surrounded by light. When at last he opened his eyes, his first words were, 'Wow. I feel so good, so complete, I feel whole for the first time in years and years.'

The young man was suffering from what is commonly referred to as a fragmented soul, whereby part of his soul had become separated and isolated by his mind. In extreme cases, a person can become so disconnected from their soul and there is so much fear between the soul and their personality, it can seem as though the person has lost their soul completely. Once this happens there are no depths to which that person will not drop. They will have lost all sense of right and wrong and have no love and compassion for either themselves or humanity. They will be able to perform evil acts without a care in the world. When this person dies their soul is condemned to a miserable existence in a hell of their own making, beset by demons and fears.

Fortunately, this situation occurs infrequently, but I mention it to remind you that such a person lives in a world without joy. They may look for happiness, as we all do, but they will seek it through hurting others or fulfilling their baser desires, neither of which can bring them the satisfaction that they seek. All souls seek happiness however damaged they may be, but many look in the wrong places. They look for happiness in the material world when it can only be found within oneself.

Happiness is not found; it is created within.

To complete your soul connection I would like you to work through the following soul connection exercise – a meditation that gives you a vehicle to take you symbolically on the final stages of your journey. As with all self-healing work, the two most important ingredients are intent and love. If we have a positive intent to connect and the love for ourselves to enable it, then we can take this special and sacred step.

In this meditation I shall be referring to a crystal cord that connects our soul to our human form. This cord stays attached to our spirit throughout our life and only disconnects when we die. Since our spirit is always linked to us via this connection, there are times when it can leave our body for a period of time. This generally happens at night. The process in which we deliberately and consciously let our spirit roam free is called astral travelling, and it can lead us to many amazing experiences. I shall not be discussing astral travelling in any more detail here but there are many books available on the subject (see *Life after Death and the World Beyond* in Further Reading, *page 258*).

## SYMBOL FOR SOUL CONNECTION
The symbol on the following page will raise your vibration and help you connect with your soul. Use it with the meditation for soul connection that follows. It is sacred and has been used in various forms by Buddhists and Hindus for centuries.

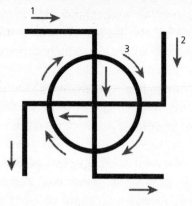

*To draw the soul-connection symbol start with the first down-ward stroke, like a zed, then go above to make the second stroke, and finally draw the circle in a clockwise direction.*

EXERCISE: MAKE YOUR SOUL CONNECTION

- Find a quiet place where you won't be disturbed.
- Close your eyes and breathe in deeply four times.
- See roots growing out of your feet deep into the ground beneath you.
- Visualise the roots growing all the way down into the centre of the Earth, grounding you completely.
- Feel yourself become very, very small.
- Step into your heart centre – your heart chakra in the centre of your chest.
- When you have stepped into your heart chakra, imagine a chamber filled with pink light and see a crystal cord that leads upwards.
- Feel that you are in a loving place and feel a great sense of calm. Know that you are positive and courageous.
- Draw the symbol for soul connection and see it spinning. Follow it upwards as you travel up the crystal cord.

- Continue travelling higher and higher up the cord. Pass through all the higher chakras until you come through your crown chakra, which will appear to you as a lotus – a huge water lily.
- Continue your journey up the cord.
- Come to a bright light and stop here. You are at the point of unconditional love – Christ's consciousness.
- Connect to the wonderful energy of Jesus, who represents unconditional love. Know yourself to be in a total state of non-judgemental love and respect.
- Take a few moments to consider yourself in this light. If you wish, you can communicate with Jesus. Feel yourself loving and respecting all that you know, including yourself. If there is anyone in your life who you still have an issue with, forgive them and love them.
- Now see a white dove. This dove represents the Holy Spirit – the essence of the divine – and will lead you the rest of the way. Follow this beautiful bird further up the crystal cord.
- Come into a space of great light. Coming from the light in front of you, see an image of yourself, pure and filled with light. This is your soul and as such it is unaffected by the worries of daily life. It is full of wisdom and is waiting to reunite with you.
- Step forward and become one with your soul.
- Feel yourself being uplifted and filled with peace and calm. Take some time to savour the moment.
- When you are ready, make your descent along the crystal cord in your own time, and quietly, quietly come into your heart space. Sit for a while and just listen to your heartbeat, then come back into the room.

This is the story of an American woman who attended one of my workshops in New York. She had already attended a couple of my classes and I had felt a bond developing between us as she had started to relax with me. This woman's life had been filled with abuse, from her childhood and through two marriages – in each she had received dreadful physical and mental abuse. She was now free of all of them but still working on her self-healing. She was determined to succeed but life was still difficult, and as she put it, 'I feel so lonely inside'.

This hole inside her, this great pit of loneliness that seemed to envelop her completely, was drawing her back towards unsuitable partners. She was so needy that she was vulnerable. She attracted men who were also damaged and who very often showed anger and frustration with violence. She spoke to me of her inner loneliness and the need for something or someone that she could not define.

The workshop was based on soul connection, and I had taken this woman and the rest of the group through the healing work as I have set it out in this chapter. When we finished the guided meditation on soul connection, she sat with tears running down her cheeks, her eyes shining and her face filled with a great look of joy. She told me that she had started to follow the crystal cord but had felt great fear, just as she always did when she was on the point of surrendering and letting herself go towards the divine. But this time she had reassured herself with the thought that she knew me and could trust me, so it was OK to let herself go. Even before I had led her and the rest of the class to see their image in front of them, she said that she had seen herself reflected 'like a twin soul'. This aspect of her being was pure and untouched by the events of her life. Once the two of them merged she had felt a great feeling of completeness as she became one and whole again.

When this woman was young and abused she had become separated from her soul, and that was why she had the feeling of loneliness. She performed a great healing on herself that day in the workshop because she had reunited herself with her soul after so many years of unhappiness. She had worked extremely hard to make this happen – to overcome her lack of self-esteem and trust – and it was a great joy to see her make this amazing transition. After making her soul connection, she no longer felt the dark hole inside her. She certainly looked radiant and full of joy as a result of the experience.

## Evolvement and Enlightenment

As our life evolves so our soul gains power and strength from the traumas, challenges and events that we experience. The ultimate aim of our soul is to be completely reunited with its source – with God. For this to happen our soul needs to be at a sufficiently high vibration. The process of reuniting is called enlightenment: being light enough to be at one with God. Until we have reached this state we keep returning to Earth for more of life's challenges, so that we can continue with our spiritual growth and evolution.

People often ask me how I can tell the difference between a young soul, one that is still at its earliest stages of growth, and an old soul. Without wishing to sound judgemental, my answer is that some people seem to have a greater capacity for compassion and love than others. Some souls haven't learned how to be happy. They haven't learned yet that happiness can never come from making others unhappy, and they are preoccupied with violence and creating misery for others. These people feel that their anger will be assuaged by revenge and inflicting hurt on other people.

If we can see the obsession of such people with the darker side of life not as evil, but as a stage of development, it can help us make a little more sense of the ways of the world. This understanding can help us be more tolerant of behaviour that seems completely senseless. We need the darkness and 'evil' to show us the power and strength of the light. However, I don't believe we are meant to dwell in the dark, but only to stop there a while to notice and observe. We can then move to the light by preference, and eventually all souls will evolve to this understanding. All souls are equal; they are just at different stages of their journey back home. Tolerance and compassion are the keys for our mutual co-existence.

---

Love travels on the wings of our thoughts so that we can heal others with our love, wherever they are.

---

## Distance Healing

As I come towards the end of this book and you get closer to the end of your assisted journey, I would like to introduce you to distance healing. This is a form of healing that you can do for your family and friends, or for any being you know who is in any form of distress or need. It will allow you to feel less helpless when you are either too far away or just unable to help in any practical way.

In addition, I see distance healing as a great tool to help our planet Earth as she goes through these difficult times and suffers so much from global warming, the greenhouse effect, the devastation of her forests and the pollution of her waters and air. You can also step into the universal energy stream you will be creating and gain the benefit of its powerful healing properties through love and light.

To achieve this healing we utilise the mind, which we have discovered has immense power, to manifest our intent. We harness the energy of our thoughts so as to make unbelievable changes not only in our own lives but also in the lives of those about us.

Use your love and intent to heal in the following meditation. Combine these two qualities with your imagination and the power of visualisation and you can change the world!

---

EXERCISE: PLANETARY HEALING

- Find a quiet place where you won't be disturbed, then close your eyes and breathe in deeply four times.
- Visualise your roots going deep into the ground beneath your feet.
- See golden light all around you.
- Now see a beam of white light coming down from the skies, powered by the energies of divine love. See the light entering your crown chakra and feel it filling you with healing light.
- Pause while you feel the healing.
- Now see beams of this light leave your heart chakra and surround those to whom you wish to send love and healing.
- Pause while the light makes its outward journey.
- See the planet Earth spinning slowly in your hands.

See light and love from your heart surrounding the Earth. See the globe spinning in golden light.

- Send light and love to fill the seas and rivers of the world. See sparkling water turning from azure and aquamarine to the deepest indigo in the vast oceans. See the colours become stronger and clearer as the water is healed and becomes clear of toxins and pollutants.
- Pause.
- Send love and light to all the animals and birds of the world. See wild animals running free, unharmed by humankind, and see domestic animals treated with respect and care. See all animals and birds free from abuse, free from hunger and flourishing in a world free from hate and fear.
- Pause.
- Send love and light to the plants of the world. See the vegetable kingdom flourishing and the great forests growing, untouched by humans. See the plants and vegetables we need growing in pure soil that holds no trace of pollution. See all this in a world without fear and a world without hate.
- Pause.
- Send love and light to every child, woman and man in the world. See them living in love and harmony. See humanity free from hunger, free from fear and in peace.
- See the planet spinning in a bright light and know that every single living thing that lives upon her great lands and in her vast seas is healed.
- Pause.
- See everyone you know who needs help in any way standing in front of you in this great light.
- Pause.
- Now put yourself into this healing light.

- Pause.
- Bring your hands to your heart and feel the love in every cell of your body.
- Pause.
- Open your eyes and gently and slowly come back into the room.

Thank you and bless you, Anne.

---

The following event occurred after a planetary meditation I led with a great group in Singapore. Dolphins are very special creatures. They have been on Earth for an immense amount of time and appear to be endowed with immense wisdom. They also seem to have a great love for humans.

It was the end of an exceptionally bonding and loving workshop in Singapore, hosted by my friend Suzie who in her amazing open-hearted and generous way had treated us to *haute cuisine* and shared her lovely home. We had all bonded so well; we had cried, laughed and shared many inner hopes, fears and much love.

On the final day of the workshop I led us all through a planetary healing and, at Suzie's request, sent a special message of love and healing to all the dolphins of the world. 'I love dolphins,' Suzie had told me. 'It would be a dream come true to swim with them.' We had a beautiful healing meditation and the dolphins were duly included. Then we said our fond farewells and the next morning I went off to the airport.

I had a long wait as my plane was delayed by two hours but I felt so loved and warm that I didn't mind at all. I just sat and soaked up all the wonderful energies that I could feel wrapping around me. I felt so good I thought someone must be thinking of me and sending love.

The next day I had a phone call from Suzie – she was so excited she could hardly talk. The previous morning, while I had been sitting at the airport, a pod of dolphins had been sighted off the coast of Singapore, by Punggol marina. This was such a totally unexpected and surprising event that the beach was soon crowded with the local press.

Suzie and her friends had dashed down to the beach as soon as she had heard the news. When they got there, the press photographers told them that the dolphins were some way out and that they were disappointed because they couldn't get any close-ups. 'Don't worry,' Suzie had said. 'I'll call them.' She went to the edge of the sea and called out to the dolphins. Sure enough, it wasn't long before they all came swimming into the shallow waters. 'How did you do that?' asked the incredulous pressmen. 'Oh, it was easy,' Suzie said, full of smiles. 'I just told them I loved them.'

## Our Spiritual Helpers

### Angels

There are beings in the spiritual realms that are constantly helping and guiding us. We may never see them or even know of their existence but they are nevertheless very much a part of our lives. Angels are beings that are totally committed to helping humankind. They will always come when called and will come to your aid when you are in trouble. Sometimes an angel may appear as a human, who arrives just in time to rescue you from a disaster. At other times we won't see them at all, only benefit from the result of their work. But remember to call for your angels or they won't step in.

You can ask angels to help you in any number of ways. I call them in whenever I meditate or give someone a healing and ask them to create a circle of protection and love around us. When I lived in Hong Kong and London I made constant use of the taxi angel! I know people who call them to help with finding parking spaces and to assist with many everyday situations.

The archangels are the most powerful of all the angels and they are very special. Most of us have heard of the Archangel Gabriel, the messenger who is mentioned several times in the Bible, notably when foretelling the birth of Jesus. Others include the Archangel Raphael, who is the angel of healing, the Archangel Uriel and the Archangel Michael. If you are ever in real danger, call for Archangel Michael as he is the angel with the sword and has an army of supporting angels who can protect you.

## Guides

As well as angels, we have other helpers waiting to give us guidance and assistance, not only with our emergencies but also with our everyday lives. Everyone has a guide, often more than one. They exist in other realms so cannot be seen with the physical eye, but they are visible to our inner eye – in our 'imagination'. Sometimes a guide is a member of the family who has passed on. As I've said, my first guide was my grandmother. After she had been with me for a while, she told me she was leaving as she had other work to do, nursing and helping souls as they pass into heaven. I was then guided by Yellow Hawk, a Native American who is with me still. It was Yellow Hawk who taught me how to heal and gave me many of the healing symbols that I have shown you in this book.

Guides are usually very evolved beings and can come from many different spiritual cultures, not necessarily our own. It is not unusual, for example, for an English Catholic to have a Tibetan Buddhist monk as their guide, or for a Chinese to have a Christian nun. Many people have Native Americans as guides and mentors because their wisdom and knowledge of nature is helpful to us at this time, when the planet is suffering so much.

You may have already met your guide in meditation or they may have contacted you in some other way, but if you haven't or don't know who he or she is then use the meditation I am about to show you to connect with them. Have faith in the process and allow yourself to be open to this meeting. When you meet your guide, or guides, you may find that their body is indistinct and their face may have no form. Don't worry about this; accept what you see and ask for their name. You can get clues about their identity by looking at their hands, their clothes and what they are wearing on their feet. Ask them as many questions as you wish. They will have a broader picture of your life and can give you insights that may well help you on your journey.

Once you have established connection with your guide you can contact them at any time during meditation for further help and guidance. Sometimes you may find they get in touch with you when you are not meditating. On these occasions, their messages may come as insights, flashes of inspiration and the kinds of ideas that seem to come from nowhere.

EXERCISE: MEET YOUR GUIDE

- Find a quiet place.
- Close your eyes and breathe in deeply four times.
- See a beam of white light coming down from the sky and entering your crown chakra. Feel the light surround you and fill you completely.
- Let your roots grow down deep into the earth beneath you.
- Pause for a few moments while you ground yourself.
- Imagine that you are walking along a deserted beach. Feel the soft sand beneath your feet.
- Notice that above you the sky is blue and clear. Watch the seagulls wheel and hear them cry.
- Now walk down to the seashore, where the waves are breaking gently.
- Feel relaxed and calm as you walk along in the water, letting the waves caress your feet.
- Pause.
- Continue to walk down the beach and feel the warm Sun on your back. There is a slight breeze ruffling your hair and keeping you at a perfect temperature.
- Notice a figure approaching from some way away.
- Realise that this faint figure in the distance is your guide coming towards you.
- As they come nearer you can see your guide a little more clearly – can you tell if it is a man or a woman?
- As they get still closer you can see your guide's hands and feet.
- See the clothes your guide is wearing. Can you tell which era they are from?
- Your guide stops before you now and speaks, giving you a message.
- Now your guide passes you a gift that will help you

in life – acknowledge it and see the message in the symbolism of the gift.

- Ask the guide some questions and know that the first thought that comes back to you is the answer.
- When you have finished your dialogue, bid your guide farewell, knowing that this being of love is watching over you every day of your life. Your guide will give you help and guidance in everything you do by communicating with you through your thoughts, ideas, inspiration and intuitive feelings.
- Leave the beach now and make your way back into the room with the knowledge that you are never alone.

---

## Our Spirit is Our Strength

Now we've come to the end of the book, I would like to leave you with the assurance that no matter what illness you have been suffering, whether it be physical, emotional or mental, you will be able to overcome the worst of it if you have the determination and resolve. You may still feel the pain and you may be disabled by it in some way, but if you allow your spirit to be strong you will no longer be its victim.

I shall close by sharing with you this account of the recent illness of a friend of mine, Vernon Simmonds. Vernon is a man of great character and through his experience I wish to show you that our spirit allows us to overcome the challenges in our lives. It is never too late to listen to your angel!

Vernon Churchill Simmonds was a Battle of Britain pilot. He spent his war flying Hurricanes and Spitfires.

Now he is over eighty years old, and lives in my village of Burley in the New Forest. The year 2000 was a very busy one for Vernon as he was involved in the sixtieth anniversary celebrations of the Battle of Britain and so was called to many meetings and official functions, and made various television appearances. He and the few of his pilot friends who were still living found these occasions quite draining and reliving the events of the past affected them all.

Old emotions resurfaced and Vernon was disturbed by dreams and recollections that came back to haunt him. These traumatic memories resulted in him becoming very ill and he was told that he would need a heart valve operation in November 2000. He refused to agree to it, saying he had done enough in his life and was ready to go. Vernon was content to call it a day; he had had several spells in hospital over the years and he didn't have the will to go through another one. His family were concerned and, although they understood and respected his feelings, wished that he would have the operation that could save his life.

Then one morning in February, Vernon called his wife Shirley and told her he had been talking to his guardian angel! His angel had told him that he could go if he wanted to, but that there was still work for him to do. Vernon contemplated this for a while and then decided that he would heed his angel's advice and have the operation. So he went ahead, even though the surgeon feared that he might have left it too late. He seemed to make a successful recovery and once he got home he spent his time doing work for charity and putting all his affairs in order.

Vernon now felt that he had completed his life's work, so when he was rushed to hospital four months later he really thought that it was the end. He suffered a massive haemorrhage that could not be contained. Although he was rushed to another hospital with better facilities, his family were informed that he only had hours to go. He had over eight pints of transfused blood in the space of twenty-four hours. As he watched his lifeblood and strength pulsing away from him, Vernon longed to leave it all behind. However, as he lay there his angel came to visit him once again. She told him that he still had unfinished work to do, and so he would recover. Within an hour the haemorrhage had ended.

Vernon spent his recovery time in hospital doing what he could for his fellow patients and also encouraging the nursing staff. Many of them felt that their work was not appreciated and he spent hours praising them for their efforts and encouraging them through the day. He was at hand to help one of his fellow war heroes pass over. He was busier than ever! He has now returned home and is actively helping others. His spirit is strong. His tenacity and his appetite for life is a wonderful example for us all.

Blessings and love.
Anne Jones.

# Postscript

I hope that I have given you a good start to your healing journey towards spiritual, mental, emotional and physical wellbeing. Through the events of my own life, and my changing expectations and perceptions, I have evolved a credo that has brought me immense and lasting happiness. From the understanding I have gained from these experiences, I offer you a personal spirituality that has no rules and regulations and which will allow you to find your own way to connect to your soul, your inner wisdom and the divine. Armed with this personal philosophy we can follow our own truth and let go of our limitations.

It is time for us to take our power into our own hands by taking full responsibility for ourselves and the way we live, think and value ourselves and others. It is time to look for peace and happiness within instead of relying on others to create it for us.

Set your mind to that which you desire and, working from your heart, hold your intent clearly and strongly. You will be amazed at how your life will be transformed. There are no limits!

# Further Reading

Jack Angelo, *Your Healing Power*, Piatkus, 1994

Barbara Ann Brennan, *Hands of Light*, Bantam Press, 1990

Lama Surya Das, *Awakening to the Sacred*, Bantam Press, 2000

Betty Eadie, *Embraced by the Light*, HarperCollins, 1995

Theo Gimbel, *Healing Colour*, Gaia Books, 2001

Louise Hay, *You Can Heal Your Life,* Hay House, 2000

Peter Hough and Jenny Randles, *Life after Death and the World Beyond*, Piatkus, 1999

Susan Jeffers, *Dare to Connect*, Piatkus, 1995

Susan Jeffers, *Feel the Fear and Do it Anyway*, Arrow Books, 1991

Brian Keenan, *An Evil Cradling*, Vintage, 1993

Matthew Manning, *The Healing Journey*, Piatkus, 2001

Bote Mikkers, *The Pendulum Workbook*, Ashgrove Press, 1998

Debbie Shapiro, *The Bodymind Workbook*, Houghton Mifflin, 1990

Debbie Shapiro, *Your Body Speaks Your Mind*, Piatkus, 1996

Betty Shine, *Mind to Mind*, Corgi Books, 1989

Betty Shine, *Mind Magic*, Corgi Books, 1992

Betty Shine, *Mind Waves*, Corgi Books, 1993

Howard and Dorothy Sun, *Colour Your Life*, Piatkus, 2001

Eckhart Tolle, *The Power of Now*, Hodder Headline, 2001

Neale Donald Walsch, *Conversations with God*, Hodder & Stoughton, 1996

Ruth White, *Chakras*, Piatkus, 1998

Ruth White, *Working with Your Chakras*, Piatkus, 1993

Stuart Wilde *Affirmations*, Hay House, 1989

Paul Wilson, *Instant Calm*, Penguin Books, 1995

Hearts and Hands
*Healing with Love and Compassion*

---

Hearts and Hands is a non-profit-making organisation that is dedicated to spreading the understanding of natural healing throughout the world. Please contact us at Hearts and Hands if you wish to purchase a CD of the guided meditations in this book, or if you would like help with the contents – either as an individual or on a group basis. We have trained facilitators and healers throughout the world who can lead, guide, teach and support you. For further information on our workshops and meditation meetings please contact us at Hearts and Hands Healing in the UK: 21 Honey Lane, Burley, Ringwood, Hampshire BH24 4EN, or visit our website www.heartshands.org, or email us at care@heartshands.org

Hearts and Hands have representatives and teachers in the following countries: UK, USA, Malaysia, Roumania, Singapore, Hong Kong, Russia, South Africa and Australia. Please contact Hearts and Hands in the UK for names and contact numbers.

## Healing Network

If you need healing for yourself or your family and friends, or if you would like to join us in sending distance healing to those in need, please email us at care@heartshands.org

# Index